31 EDIBLE WILD PLANTS

ABSOLUTELY ANYONE

CAN FIND IN NORTH AMERICA

A BEGINNER'S GUIDE TO
SAFE AND SUCCESSFUL FORAGING

HADASSAH LEWIS

CONTENTS

Part I
THE EMERGING FORAGER IN YOU

Part II
INTO THE WILD GREEN BEYOND

PREFACE

Do you think of foraging as more of an essential skill or a trending hobby? Could edible wild plants be key to our wellbeing and survival? Please understand, I am not a conspiracy theorist or doom-sayer, but an optimistic person who looks for the bright side.

But let's be real. In 2018, if someone had told you that, in 2020, North Americans would spend months sequestered at home, anxious about accessibility to toilet paper and food, would you have believed them?

Neither would I. But it happened.

So, are shortages such a big deal everywhere?

I had the privilege of living in the Amazon rainforest for five years, invited by an indigenous community.

This people group maintains much of their original culture but has also chosen to adopt many conveniences from the outside world.

For example, my indigenous friends sweeten coffee with sugar, eat rice, and use processed oil. But they also boil manioc root they planted, eat wild game, and snack on fruit gathered from trees or bushes.

Food shortages aren't as problematic in the rainforest as they are in cities. Although my friends complained about the skyrocketing rice prices in 2020, they had the option of using root vegetables as their staple carbohydrate. Even if crops were destroyed by wild pigs, foraging in the jungle would allow them to survive. For generations, mothers and fathers and grandparents have passed on valuable knowledge about the edible wild foods that sustain life and preserve health.

Besides the practical and sustainable aspect of this way of life, I was inspired by my friends' attitude of gratitude and respect for the jungle's bounty. They understand nature and are deeply connected with its rhythms.

In becoming part of this beautiful community, I learned about jungle foraging and was reminded of my roots, having grown up in a rural farming community, with constant opportunities to explore fields and forests.

Certain childhood memories began to stir my heart and imagination again.

My dad's excitement when one of the weeds in our garden was lambsquarters.
Foraging for fiddleheads with friends in early spring.
Leisurely afternoons spent with my mom and siblings in the woods, carrying multiple identification guides to observe flowers, trees, and birds.

How had I allowed adult responsibilities and pressures of modern life to steal too much time and distract me from the joys of nature?

PREFACE

Living in North America again, I see our world with a new perspective. For example, hiking with family members has always seemed like a normal outdoor activity.

But now, I imagine the confused reaction if my indigenous friends could see my brother and I after 10 hours on forest trails. "Why on earth would two intelligent human beings spend a whole day in the woods and come back empty-handed?" they would ask each other. "Didn't they see all those plants with edible fruits and leaves and roots?"

In their opinion, that would be a failure of a hike. They'd probably feel a combination of amusement and sympathy for their poor, incompetent North American friends who left the woods hungry and had to buy groceries on the way home.

And, to tell you the truth, it makes me laugh too.

So, I decided to study wild plants in North America and learn how to safely identify and harvest the edible ones. It is a rewarding and fun path that I plan to continue traveling.

My indigenous friends would be delighted to see how often I return from a hike with some kind of wild food in hand. I've introduced my young nieces and nephews to the joy of foraging and my dependence on processed foods has decreased.

Foraging is not an unattainable skill inherent to select cultural groups. Absolutely anyone can learn to safely identify, harvest and prepare edible wild plants. I hope that the information here inspires you and helps develop the confidence and abilities you need to be a successful forager.

This book is your invitation to join me on a path of adventure and discovery that leads to edible wild plants, a deeper understanding of nature, and so much more.

- Taking into account the different terminologies used in both the U.S. and Canada, the term "Indigenous Americans" refers to Native Americans or American First Peoples.
- Following the introduction is a glossary, which includes many botanical terms used in this book and others you will probably come across as you research edible plants.

FREE BONUS GIFT!

Especially during my first spring and summer of serious foraging, it was always hard to resist the urge to take five or six (or ten!) foraging books in my backpack. Before harvesting plants, I wanted to identify them correctly by looking at photos while still in the woods or field. This is a rather heavy dilemma that I want to help you avoid.

So that you can leave this book at home but still take advantage of the photos and botanical illustrations while foraging, I have designed a special gift just for you!

31 Edible Wild Plants: Forager's Field Notes and Photo Guide is ready for you to download, print, and take along on your next expedition in the great outdoors!

This free printable contains a photo and sketch for each of the 31 plants featured in this book. That way, you can refer to it while foraging for help with plant identification. Also, every other page of the printable is lined, providing space to take notes about the characteristics of each plant, where you find it, and how you decide to cook or prepare it.

On page 115 is a QR code and link to access **31 Edible Wild Plants: Forager's Field Notes and Photo Guide.**

INTRODUCTION

If you are reading the paperback version and would like to see all the photos from part 1 in color, you can access them at the link below, or by scanning this QR code with your phone.

https://bit.ly/
Part1photos_31EWP

A children's song talks of a day when teddy bears go down to the woods to picnic in secret. The bears eat delicious foods and play hide and seek. Equally enthusiastic, foragers head out beneath bright blue skies or even on overcast days to find and harvest tasty natural foods.

We discover hidden places beside sparkling streams where fiddleheads and marsh marigolds grow. We venture into leafy forest glades to pick elderberries and gather fallen nutlets beneath basswood trees. We wade into chilly water to find arrowroot tubers and harvest cattail stems. We meander through dappled woodlands, seeking clearings where nutritious but prickly stinging nettles grow. We spend hours picking rose hips just because we found a recipe for rose hip jam or salve. We brave the heat in arid climates and follow desert creatures to find sheep sorrel and purslane. We'll comb vacant lots for "weeds" like plantain and chickweed or find stands of ripe lambsquarters to winnow into grain.

As we explore the landscape, we delight in secret glimpses into nature's beauty. Birds flit among the trees, squirrels scurry through fall leaves, and a doe watches us shyly. Shimmering fish dart through mountain pools and nibble on our toes. Herons fly off when we forage in the shallows, while butterflies dance around us as we dry off in the sun.

We return triumphantly from our outings, sometimes sunburned, wet, and muddy, but almost always with a harvest gathered to enhance a salad, cook as a vegetable, or flavor a soup. We make delicious jam after a bumper blackberry harvest or brew coffee from chicory roots. And as we take nature's bounty from our baskets, we wonder why more people don't harvest food from the wild.

INTRODUCTION

After all, foragers are in their element when busy collecting spring leaves or flowers, digging for edible roots, or munching wild nuts for lunch. Yet the closest most North Americans have probably gotten to foraging is picking blackberries. One reason might be that around 55% of the world's human population is urbanized and has largely forgotten the art of foraging (United Nations, 2021).

Because most of our food is mass-produced, cultivated on huge monoculture farms, and highly processed before being packaged and transported to stores, we don't need to depend directly on nature. As a result, most people would have no clue where to start harvesting wild foods and might find them unpalatable.

But times have changed. In recent years, and especially since the pandemic hit, scarcity has been seeping into our lives. As a result, more people are seriously considering going off-grid, moving into tiny houses, and living off the land.

FORAGING: BACK TO OUR ROOTS

Foraging is the practice of seeking, identifying, and collecting wild foods for sustenance, medicine, and more. Uncultivated, these wild foods, such as mushrooms, berries, underground vegetables, and weeds, grow naturally.

Foraging is not a new invention or trending survival technique. There was a time when everyone was a forager by default. If you didn't hunt or forage, you didn't eat. It was that simple. Hunter-gatherer societies included Indigenous Americans (both North and South), southern Africa's Koi-San, and Australia's Aborigines. These cultures depended on and revered nature, acknowledging that they would be lost without it.

Even in agricultural societies thousands of years ago, supplementing farmed produce with wild foods was a typical way of life. Jam, preserves, wine, and flavored vinegar all included local ingredients. Yet plants that once provided nutritious additions to the dinner table are now regarded as "weeds" and resolutely removed from gardens.

The prevalence of supermarkets, technology, and convenience foods contributed to these extensive changes. As a result, even most Indigenous Americans cultures, once experts at living off the land, rely less on the ancient art of foraging, utilizing modern methods to meet their basic needs.

Another contributor to the demise of foraging is society's increasing disconnection from nature. Nearly everything is mass-produced or synthetically manufactured. For example, the active ingredient in many painkillers naturally occurs in plants such as chamomile or willow. However, having discovered how to isolate the chemical compounds, drug manufacturers now produce painkillers synthetically.

Few people venture into nature these days to encounter wide open skies, peaceful woods, bubbling streams, or endless prairies. Those who do rediscover an essential connection with nature while enjoying outdoor activities. We are not separate from nature but intimately connected with it. If the natural world collapses, so will we. Scientists believe we are experiencing the sixth big extinction. To those who rely on nature's resources to some degree, the disappearance of even one living creature is a substantial loss (Begum, 2021).

It seems extinction might be inevitable, though, since many people rely on cities for all their needs, including food. Some children firmly believe that milk comes from cartons and carrots originate in bags. They have never planted seeds or watched plants grow, are afraid of the sun, and refuse to lie on the grass because they have been taught that it's dirty.

Modern technology is a major culprit in keeping people away from nature. Smartphones and apps excite the dopamine centers in our brains, triggering cravings that lead to addiction. But some people still know that nature can be exciting too. Exercise releases endorphins, stimulating the brain's pleasure centers. Breathing fresh air, stopping to admire a wildflower, or eating blackberries straight off the bush compounds the feeling of delight.

Before the pandemic, there was little incentive to find food sources outside cities and grocery stores. Hardly anyone would consider checking a park or vacant lot to see what might be growing. Foraging is finally making a comeback, however. Besides being an enjoyable hobby, it can provide relief for hard-pressed consumers as a supplementary source of sustenance. There is growing interest in edible weeds, herbal teas, and wild fruit jam.

This resurgence in foraging is the natural result of a growing conviction that "certain certainties," to quote poet T.S. Eliot, are no longer as enduring as we thought they were (Poetry Foundation, 2020).

A TIME TO SURVIVE AND A TIME TO THRIVE

SHORTAGES AND SUPPLY CHAINS

When was the last time you saw empty shelves at your local supermarket? Perhaps this week. How much of your budget now goes toward cooking oil and gasoline, once plentiful and more affordable commodities? Global events have exposed the fragility of the complex supply chains that underpin modern life and our utter dependence on them.

Because some products travel vast distances, they are more susceptible to disruptions ranging from hurricanes to wars. Unexpected recent events have highlighted how vulnerable we are to supply chain disruptions. Some examples are the giant container ship that blocked the Suez Canal in 2021 (Yee and Goodman, 2021), fires in Chinese semiconductor factories, droughts, floods, and the Ukraine war precipitating shortages of cooking oil, wheat, and crude oil. This year, the United States experienced baby formula shortages, compounded by a significant product recall.

While we blamed product shortages on panic buying in the early phases of lockdown, empty shelves have become a daily reality that has not ended. A February 2022 survey by tech company SAP revealed the prevalence of scarcity. Sixty-seven percent of respondents believed that empty shelves and product shortages are the "new normal" (Harris, 2022). Many had been forced to switch brands due to consistent unavailability and were concerned about future shortages of food, hygiene products, and prescription medication.

In light of this, many consumers, perhaps including you, would like to take more control over their everyday lives.

WHATEVER THE WEATHER

Despite the claims of those who deny climate change, it's now indisputable that something is amiss with the weather. Perhaps you have sweltered through a scorching summer or had to evacuate because your property lay in the path of a hurricane or a rampant wildfire. If so, you know first-hand that the climate is not the same as it used to be. Formerly cold regions like Alaska and British Columbia have documented record-high temperatures. Dangerous wildfires precipitated by extreme heat have caused fatalities and damaged large areas of land in California and Australia. Meanwhile, devastating floods have swept away homes, businesses, and infrastructure in Asia, Europe, and southern Africa.

Extreme heat generates tropical storms because heat is stored in vast oceans like the Pacific. Intense storms have negatively impacted major cities like New York and much of the southeastern U.S. coast, resulting in economic disruption and infrastructure damage. These storms also have catastrophic impacts on agriculture. Animals are drowned, planting dates are delayed, and harvests are destroyed.

FOOD SAFETY

Do you really know what you're eating? A famous experiment demonstrated that a meal from a fast-food restaurant was so riddled with preservatives that it did not spoil for years. Processed foods, in particular, contain numerous additives identified only by mysterious E numbers.

Food safety is an additional concern. According to the U.S. Food and Drug Administration (2022), food recalls in the first half of 2022 included processed foods ranging from canned soups and seafood products to ice cream and peanut butter. Disease-causing bacteria such as salmonella contaminated many products.

The problem is not confined to the United States. In South Africa, after numerous consumers were hospitalized in 2019, a food processing company recalled nearly all its processed meat products due to contamination by listeria bacteria (Marler, 2019).

NATURAL PROVISION

Despite appearances, foraging is about more than prepping. It is about connecting with nature and developing new skills. The knowledge and ability to find and harvest wild foods will make you less vulnerable to future shocks like shortages and climate change. It will also empower you to take more control over your health by eating plants produced naturally in the wild rather than foods that were produced synthetically in factories.

If you're so new to foraging that the concept seems unusual, consider these scenarios. Have you ever caught a fish and grilled it? Have you harvested and eaten mussels at the seashore? Have you picked wild berries, made tea from dandelion leaves, or built a fire with wood gathered from the woods? If you have, then you're already a forager in the making.

But even if you haven't done any of these things, don't worry. This book will show you how to succeed on your path to becoming a forager. First, in part one, you will learn some foraging basics and general plant types. Then, in the second part of this book, you will find in-depth information about 31 of the most common edible wild plants in North America and how to use them. This will equip you to safely identify them on your expeditions into nature.

DISCLAIMER

The information contained in this book is for informative purposes only. Although great care has been taken to provide reliable, accurate information, you are responsible for researching and verifying the facts provided in this book.

The author and sources are not qualified botanists, horticulturalists, or healthcare practitioners. However, we are people who are passionate about foraging, edible wild foods, and sustainable living.

Especially if you are a beginner, the author strongly recommends you forage with more experienced people. Many plants and fungi cause sickness or are deadly if consumed. Additionally, any food eaten for the first time, even if adequately identified and safe for consumption, could cause an unusual reaction for some people. It is your responsibility to ensure that you are harvesting and using the correct plant, and it is your choice whether or not to try new foods. The author cannot be held responsible for incorrect plant identification or adverse reactions to edible wild plants you are unaccustomed to.

Any information on traditional health care or botanical remedies is not intended to be a substitute for medical treatment by qualified health practitioners. Always consult your doctor or healthcare provider before using any natural remedies mentioned in this book. This is especially vital if you have a known medical condition or are pregnant or breastfeeding.

GLOSSARY

 He plants trees to benefit another generation.

— CAECILIUS STATIUS

Achene: Small, one-seeded nutlet formed from a single carpel, shed in fruit without releasing the seed.

Acuminate: Narrowing gradually to a point.

Acute: Sharply pointed.

Adpressed: Lying flat, closely pressed against a surface.

Aggregate species: Group of closely related micro-species, treated as one species for identification, e.g., berries, hawthorns, and dandelions.

Alternate: Leaf arrangement where leaves occur singly at nodes and not as opposite pairs.

Angiosperm: Flowering plants with seeds fully enclosed by a fruit, as opposed to gymnosperms that bear naked seeds in a cone.

Annual: Plant that completes its life cycle in one year.

Axil: Angle formed between the leaf, leaf stalk, and the stem from which it grows.

Axis: Main or central stem of a plant or inflorescence.

Blade: The expanded part of a leaf. In grasses, the part above the sheath.

Bracts: A leaf, usually much reduced or modified, that extends under and supports or enfolds a flower or inflorescence in its axis.

Bulbs: Underground stem or storage organ, usually covered with fleshy scale leaves, containing next year's plant.

Bulbil: A small bulb.

Calyx: The outermost series of floral parts, which are often green and resemble leaves.

Callus: The developing, protective wound tissue produced by a plant on any damaged surface.

Chlorophyll: Plant pigment that gives them their green color. Chlorophyll consists of photosynthetic molecules that convert light energy into chemical energy.

Chloroplast: An organelle within plant cells that is responsible for photosynthesis and contains chlorophyll pigment.

Chlorosis: The symptom of a plant disease or disorder, where they lose their green color. Such plants are pale green or yellow. Chlorosis is usually caused by an interruption in the processes that create chlorophyll such as nutrient deficiencies or insufficient light.

Crenate: With rounded teeth or lobes; scalloped.

Compound: Flowers or leaves which have two or more parts.

Deciduous: Perennial plants that lose their leaves in winter.

Decurrent: Leaves or mushroom gills that run down and are attached to the stem or stipe.

Dentate: Toothed, with acute teeth facing outwards.

Diffusion: Movement of molecules from a region of higher, to a region of lower solute concentration as a result of their random thermal movement.

Entire leaf: Leaf without any teeth on its edge.

Filament: The stalk of an anther. Together they comprise a stamen.

Flower: The reproductive structure of flowering plants. If fertilized, fruit and/or seeds will be produced.

Fruit: The seed-containing product of a plant.

Gene: The fundamental, physical unit of heredity.

Genotype: The genetic constitution of an organism, as opposed to its physical appearance.

Germination: When the baby root (radicle) breaks through the seed coat. A seed has "germinated" when the cotyledons (seed leaves) are fully opened. This is sometimes after a period of dormancy, awaiting suitable environmental conditions.

Habitat: The environmental conditions or place where a plant naturally grows, e.g., grassland, tundra, and forest.

Hybrid: Plant produced by cross-pollinating two different species or subspecies. Hybrids may be fertile or sterile.

Inflorescence: A flowering structure comprising more than one flower.

Mature: A plant that can reproduce.

Mulch: A loose surface soil layer, either natural or manmade, composed of organic or mineral materials. It protects the soil and plant roots from rain, temperature changes, and evaporation.

Opposite: Arrangement of leaves where they occur in pairs, one on either side of a node.

Petiole: Leaf stalk.

Phosphorus (P): An element vital for plant growth, needed for the root, DNA, and many metabolic functions. Deficiency leads to leaf discoloration. It is water soluble, and leaches easily from the soil.

Photosynthesis: The reduction of atmospheric carbon dioxide to carbohydrates. This occurs within specialized plant cells that use light as an energy source and chlorophyll as a catalyst.

Pigment: Compound that produces color in organisms.

Regeneration: Initiation and growth of any missing parts on propagated material, e.g., stem cutting, to create a complete plant.

Relative humidity: The amount of water vapor in the atmosphere, relative to it being saturated, at a particular temperature.

Reniform: Kidney-shaped leaf.

Root: The descending axis or stem of a plant anchoring the plant in the soil. Roots absorb water and nutrients from the soil.

Sapwood: The heart of the active xylem cells (used to transport water and nutrients through the plant), next to the dead cells. They are distinguished by their darker color.

Semi-evergreen: When plants fall between evergreen and deciduous. Such plants either shed their leaves for a very short time in late winter, rejuvenating quickly in spring, or lose most of their foliage for a very short time during the year. Plants may also become semi-evergreen as a result of environmental conditions like droughts.

Simple leaf: A leaf not divided into leaflets.

Succulent: Having fleshy, thick leaves or stems suited to storing water. Commonly seen in plant species which live in arid zones.

Terminal bud: The bud that terminates growth at the top of stems, resting throughout the dormant season.

Union: The place where a rootstock and scion (young shoot or twig) join in a graft to grow and develop as a whole.

Vascular bundle: Longitudinal strands of xylem and phloem connecting tissue, essential for the transport of water and solutes through the organism. It also helps provide structural support to the plant.

Vein: A vascular bundle or group of vascular bundles lying in close proximity in a leaf; the ribs of a leaf.

Water Stress: A variable condition where a plant loses more water than it takes up. This can result in increased ethylene production which further inhibits water uptake, increasing water stress.

Weed: A plant opportunistically taking advantage of suitable conditions after being distributed through human intervention. A plant out of place, competing for nutrients, water, and light.

Whorl: Variable group of three or more flowers, bracts, or any other ringed floral stem arrangement.

PART I
THE EMERGING FORAGER IN YOU

Imagine discovering a whole new world where you are off the grid and self-sufficient. You would provide your own electricity and water, embrace a simpler life, and enjoy the peace and joy of experiencing nature more deeply.

What would it be like to increase your physical activity and improve your health? How would it feel to be immersed in the changing seasons, find wild honey, and harvest native fruit, nuts, and grains? Picture yourself getting out of the house and away from the city to celebrate creation's abundance.

If you spend time in the great outdoors, you will discover endless natural wonders. Thousands of plants adorn the landscape. Trees provide shade and support wispy lichens and spongy mosses. Colorful wildflowers brighten the endless prairie. Water lilies dance on tranquil ponds while ducks sail serenely through the reeds. Delicate ferns adorn the edges of waterfalls and streams. Desert succulents bloom suddenly after rain showers. Birds gather in trees to breed and roost. Lumbering elk browse among the elms, and shy deer slip silently through shadowed forest glades.

Setting out on the path of a forager will give you unique opportunities to observe and understand nature, enriching your life and perspective.

Foraging with other people, especially when you're starting out on this journey into the world of edible wild plants, will enable you to learn from those who are more knowledgeable. As you gain experience, you too will be able to pass on what you have learned. It's always wonderful to widen your social circle and connect with like-minded people who share your passions. An added bonus is that by spending more time outdoors, you'll get extra exercise and increase your overall wellness without even trying.

SECTION 1: TAKING A NEW BUT PROVEN PATH

> *Earth was not built for six billion people all running around and being passionate about things. The world was built for about two million people foraging for roots and grubs.*

— DOUGLAS COUPLAND

I f you're considering going off-grid, foraging might be a good introduction. It's a first step to living off the land as our ancestors did.

While giant food companies offer "natural" and "organic" products, there's been a quiet revolution. People are researching food ingredients and discovering how to naturally supplement modern diets. They're supporting local community-based agriculture and farmers' markets and growing their own fresh produce. Edible wild plants play a significant role in how the local food trend has soared.

Health benefits aside, the quest for wild edibles encourages people to get outside and observe regional vegetation and yearly rhythms inherent in nature. Hardcore foragers know precisely where specific plants grow and what's available in different seasons.

Foraging provides a marvelous opportunity to learn about plants. Correct identification is essential, as is knowing when and what to harvest. Nothing compares to the achievement and delight experienced after successfully locating wild fruits, fiddleheads, or flowers to round out a meal.

MODERN FORAGING CULTURES

Despite urbanization and modern technology, eating wild-sourced foods is still taken for granted as a way of life in many communities. That shouldn't be surprising, as food is linked to national and ethnic identity. Some well-known examples are haggis in Scotland, frog legs in Thailand, and snails in France.

In addition to cultures where wild foods have been eaten for generations, there are sustainable communities that were intentionally established to rely on nature as much as possible. Japan's Konohana Family, for example, was founded in 1994 when 20 people pooled their resources and bought a 40-acre plot to start a self-sufficient, off-grid community. Today, the "family" supports about 87 individuals who cultivate over 280 types of fresh produce, rear free-range chickens, and produce honey. Except for salt, sugar, and a few spices that are purchased, the Konohana Family farm is completely self-sustaining (Tentree.com, 2017).

The Torri Superiore hamlet in Italy was constructed in the 13th century. In 1989, after being abandoned for a century, the place was rejuvenated when an off-grid community moved in permanently. Torri Superiore hosts around 400 youngsters for summer camps that promote eco-friendly living (Tentree.com, 2017).

Tinkers Bubble, an eco-village in England's rural Somerset, has drawn both permanent and temporary residents for about 21 years. Using solar, wind, and wood as energy sources eliminates the need for fossil fuels on this 40-acre property. Employment opportunities focus on forestry, gardening, and animal husbandry (Tentree.com, 2017).

The Villa Monte Reserve in Argentina covers 400 acres of native forest reserve. Residents preserve regional biodiversity by promoting sustainable living, organic farming, and forest conservation (Rejba, 2020).

Near the tiny hamlet of Haga Haga in South Africa's Eastern Cape province lies Khula Dhamma, an eco-village nestled on a 740-acre property with an indigenous forest. Solar power brings in fresh water. Khula Dhamma residents garden, raise bees, and offer permaculture workshops (Khula Dhamma, 2020).

ESSENTIAL FORAGING TIPS FOR BEGINNERS

- **Choosing the right site:** Foraging is all about location. Particularly in urban environments, it's important to choose sites that are as unpolluted as possible. Avoid roadsides and brownfields due to the high probability of contamination caused by vehicles and chemicals.
- **Obtain permission from the landowner when foraging on private land**.

- **Check for area laws or regulations.** In most North American states and provinces, you can forage sparingly on public lands like parks and nature reserves. But harvesting or picking plants is strictly prohibited in protected areas such as national parks, proclaimed nature reserves, or wilderness conservation areas. Botanical gardens may have restrictions too.
- **Start with a few plants:** Select and research one or two of the edible wild plants in this book that you hope to discover. When you successfully locate these, add a few more to your list of plants to find.
- **Get advice:** Connect with local foragers or foraging groups. They will have valuable inside information specific to your area. Ask them for tips on where and when to forage and which edible plants you can expect to find. Botanists, horticulturalists, and conservationists are great resources to assist with plant identification. Visit a nearby botanical garden to view important local plants. Some of these gardens have herbariums, which are terrific places to observe different types of plants and develop your skills in identifying them.
- **Look around you:** Every time you identify a particular plant, consider its habitat. Is it surrounded by forest, grassland, or marsh vegetation? If the plant is on a slope, is it facing north or south? Does it grow in the sun or shade, on its own or in a colony? Keep a nature diary as a personal reference guide.
- **Forage year-round:** Wild food is available throughout the year, with every season offering its own edible delights. While spring and summer foraging yield the most variety, fall brings berries, nuts, and seeds, and winter offers roots and tubers.
- **Small quantities may be sufficient:** Some plants have intense flavors, so a little goes a long way.

- **Don't overharvest:** Only take what you need. Since flowers, fruits, and seeds are the reproductive parts of a plant, taking too many could hinder the regeneration of the species. If you take more than one-third of a single plant, it could die. When harvesting bark, do not remove it from around the entire trunk. This is called ringbarking and can kill trees. Also, consider wild animals and insects. What will they do if you overharvest the plants they depend on for food?

- **Do thorough research:** Always use several sources to verify whether a plant is safe to eat, never relying on just one book or photo or smartphone app. This will protect you from stomachache, serious illness, or even death that could be caused by accidentally eating a poisonous wild plant. Proper identification is not difficult with the accessibility of books, botanical websites, and online foraging groups. It is worth investing enough time and effort to ensure you know what plants you have found. Then you can take a bite confidently, anticipating the natural goodness and flavor you are about to taste for the first time.

- **Safety first:** Make sure you are visible by wearing brightly colored or reflective clothing and hats. Forage in areas you are familiar with to avoid getting lost. It's best not to forage alone. Be aware of any dangerous snakes or other wildlife native to your region. Wear long pants in the summertime as a precaution against ticks and fleas. Use insect repellent and sunscreen as needed. Take plenty of water with you, as well as a small first-aid kit and any medications or personal items you would need in an emergency. In urban areas, leave valuables at home and forage in groups.

- **If you are not 100% certain of the identity of a plant or fungus, never eat it or give it to someone else to eat. Making sure that plants are safe for human consumption is essential to responsible foraging.**
- When researching a particular species, check how it could affect you. For example, blood pressure or appetite can be affected by substances found in wild edibles. Some plants should not be eaten by pregnant or breastfeeding women, people with certain medical conditions, or those on specific medications.
- Even after verifying a plant's edibility and ruling out risks, start slowly. Begin by eating a minimal amount of any plant or fungus the first time you collect it to ensure that you do not have any negative reaction. Common allergies to food substances such as gluten, peanuts, and apples prove that people have different physiologies. What is acceptable and healthy for one person to eat may not be safe for another.
- Anyone can have an allergic or unwelcome reaction to any plant or plant part. Your taste buds will often alert you if a new food will disagree with you. If the first nibble tastes bad, spit it out and find another type of edible plant to try.
- Listen to your body instead of mistakenly assuming that "wild is always good." For example, if you feel light-headed or develop headaches, intestinal cramps, an upset stomach, or nausea after eating a wild plant, avoid it in the future.
- Some plants and their parts are only edible during certain times in their growing cycles. Therefore, as a general guideline, harvest ripe plant parts, which are typically more palatable and safer for consumption.
- Some plants need to be cooked to deactivate toxic compounds, soften spines, or relieve bitterness. Make sure

you know how to prepare wild foods to derive maximum enjoyment and avoid unpleasant surprises.

- Fungi are problematic. Even safe, edible species may cause allergic reactions in some people. Always cook mushrooms and edible fungi thoroughly and separately from other foods before eating.

As long as you follow these guidelines, you can confidently head into the nearest field, forest, or marsh, knowing you are doing your part to stay safe, care for the environment, and practice sustainability.

The next section of this book is like an outdoor shopping trip. You will walk down the aisles of nature's grocery store by reading about the marvelous variety of plant types and plant parts that that can be foraged and eaten.

SECTION 2: A MIGHTY MULTITUDE OF MARVELS

66 *In all things of nature, there is something of the marvelous.*

— ARISTOTLE

Wherever you venture, it is truly astounding to see the abundance of edible wild plants created for us to discover, study, and enjoy. In addition to the wide variety among the kinds of plants that can be foraged, most types of plant parts can be harvested and eaten, depending on the species.

In this section, you'll discover the main plant types you will find on your foraging expeditions.

Grasses and Grains

The mention of wild grass tends to conjure up images of endless prairies. Grasses are challenging to define, as diverse species have distinct growth habits and environmental requirements. The grass family, Poaceae, wins the prize of being the world's largest plant family. Poaceae includes a significant portion of the Gramineae, or grains, including many cultivated staples such as oats, wheat, barley, millet, and rice.

What are Grains?

Grains and cereals are single-seeded dry fruits, the grass "seeds". They can be classified into naked grains, such as maize, or grains with persistent husks or chaff, such as oats. Chaff is the remainder of the grass flower, while the grain stores the plant's food.

Small Grain Cereals

Barley, originally from Western Europe and the Mediterranean, has been harvested and cultivated as a winter annual since ancient times. In some cultures, barley was used to produce nutritious milk that built strong bones. In the first century A.D., early healers recommended barley porridge to relieve throat ulcers and promote convalescence (Roberts, 2012).

Wild barley is a perennial that grows in clumps. You will likely find it on roadsides throughout the United States., except in the Southeast.

The brownish hue of wild oats may catch your eye on waste ground and hillsides in midsummer, particularly in the western United

States. Oats are an ancient grain that originated in Europe, North Africa, and Asia. Cultivated oats are an important food crop in many countries.

Wild oats have browner, smaller seeds, so you'll need to gather more before processing them. The plants prefer disturbed ground and add nitrates to the soil. Since wild oats are considered agricultural weeds, you could be doing a favor for farmers by removing wild oats from their croplands!

Oats are high in protein, vitamins, minerals, and fiber. The chaff, or oat straw, builds strong bones and helps relieve ailments such as osteoporosis, recurring colds, and flu. In addition, regularly eating oatmeal reduces stress, anxiety, depression, and panic attacks.

Triticale is a hybrid grain derived from wheat and rye. It is frost-hardy in winter and should be harvested in spring. It is shorter than rye, grows faster than barley, and is resistant to barley stripe disease.

Wild Grains for Foragers

Wild grains are "uncultivated grains that grow naturally and have for years been used as a source of sustenance" (Selinger, 2021). Wild grains need to be processed before consumption. The first step is removing the chaff. Since it is lighter than the seed, the chaff can be blown away easily, leaving the seeds behind. Curly dock seeds can be crushed and milled to make flour similar to buckwheat. Seeds from lambs-quarters, wild rye, and barnyard grass make other natural and nutritious flours. Wild rice can be eaten as a cooked grain.

Annual Grasses

Sorghum is a grass native to Africa, originating in Ethiopia. It was cultivated in Egypt about 4,000 years ago (Van Oudtshoorn, 1999). Although it was introduced to India about 1,000 years ago, it only became a significant crop in the New World in the 19th century (Van Wyk and Gericke, 2000).

Sorghum is an African staple, the only commercially grown native African cereal crop. Several cultivars are available, and they are farmed throughout Africa and beyond. Sorghum is so hardy and robust that it produces some grain even during droughts. Harvest residues are used for animal feed. Traditional African beer is brewed from malted sorghum, while sweet varieties are chewed like sugarcane. The leaves yield a red dye.

In the wild, sorghum normally grows in disturbed, damp places on the banks of streams or rivers and near marshes. In the United States, it is mainly found in the southern states.

Perennial Grasses

You'll probably find ryegrass when you forage along roadsides or in old, cultivated fields in cool areas with a lot of rainfall. One of the first grasses to be cultivated for pasture, rye prefers damp, disturbed places. There are two subspecies. Annual ryegrass lives for one growing season and perennial ryegrass regrows every spring. The two grow together in the wild and hybridize naturally.

Despite its preference for cool, damp environments, ryegrass outperforms other cultivated cereal crops on sandy, infertile soils in dry regions. Its extensive rhizome root system facilitates drought tolerance.

Important note: Ryegrass can become infected by toxic bacteria, in which case it should not be harvested. Signs of toxic bacteria include yellow mucus on the flowering part of the plant.

Legumes

Bacteria living on the roots of leguminous plants can convert atmospheric nitrogen into forms that plants can use. Rhizobia, known as nitrogen-fixing bacteria, colonize the legumes' root nodules. Rhizobia were specially designed to convert atmospheric nitrogen into ammonia, making it available to these plants. Enzymes in the root ensure that plants receive the right amount. Scientists are still establishing just how much of this nitrogen ends up in the soil and is available to the surrounding plants. Current research shows mixed results. However, it appears that when these beneficial bacteria die, the nitrogen they contain does end up in the soil.

Organic farmers and gardeners include legumes such as beans, peas, alfalfa, teff, and clover in their crop rotations to add nitrogen to the soil. These plants are grown as cover crops and used as winter feed for livestock.

Edible legumes include all peas and beans, alfalfa, teff, and clover. Eating teff powder as cereal is said to provide significant energy. White and red clover and hog peanuts are other examples of edible North American wild legumes.

Forbs (Herbs)

Forbs, or herbs, are perennial or annual plants that are herbaceous rather than woody. They are short-lived plants, often flowering, that augment other grassland species.

Some important edible forbs from the Brassica plant family include cabbages, cauliflower, kale, and mustard. Edible wild Brassicas include dandelion, plantain, curly dock, and parsnip.

Fruits and Berries

Wild fruits, produced from flowers, aid in plant reproduction by dispersing the seeds of shrubs and trees. They also feed birds and other wildlife. While berries are the most well-known, there is great diversity among wild fruits, which contain essential nutrients and vitamins.

Indigenous Americans prioritized the consumption of all kinds of edible wild fruit, including berries, which remain popular today. Nearly everyone has ventured into a vacant lot or the edge of a farm field to pick wild blueberries, blackberries, raspberries, or huckleberries. Another favorite is the wild strawberry, found on creek banks and garden borders. Native to North America, *Fragaria virginiana*, is the species from which all cultivated strawberries were bred.

Shrubs

What's the difference between trees and shrubs? Both are usually perennial, have woody stems, and regularly produce flowers, fruit, and seeds. Trees typically grow taller than 10 feet and have single trunks. Shrubs have multiple stems and are usually under 10 feet tall (Wentworth, 2013). Native shrubs may grow beneath forest trees, at the edges of pastures, or along roadsides.

Most shrubs produce berries, such as blackberries, aronia berries, and nannyberries. The abundant rose hips produced by wild roses are perfect for making jams, chutneys, and preserves. The Nootka rose, found in dappled shade in woodlands and meadows across the United States, is one of these remarkable roses.

Shoots and Stalks

A plant's shoot is comprised of all parts of the plant that grow above the ground. This includes the main stem, secondary shoots or stem branches, and leaves, together with flowers, fruit, and seeds. The word shoot is also used to refer to new growth from a node, or growth point on the main stem. These nodes are where short stems produces new leaves, usually in spring and summer when the plant is growing actively.

When foraging, gather young, tender new stems in spring while they are soft. They are usually green and don't bear many leaves. Remember that these short shoots typically bear blossoms, fruit, and seeds, so harvest them sparingly. This will enable the plant to reproduce, feeding birds, wildlife, and foragers.

Mid-spring and early summer are the best times to harvest edible stalks or tougher stalks with edible centers. Feel along the stem to determine where it becomes tender and edible instead of woody, since woody stems are rather unpalatable. Stalks toughen as they dry, so after harvesting, cook and eat them immediately, or keep them damp until you can get them into your refrigerator. For long-term storage, stalks can be canned or blanched and frozen.

Underground Vegetables

All subterranean plant parts are often referred to as roots. This can be confusing, since there are actually several distinct categories of subterranean plant parts.

A *root* is an underground extension of the plant's stem. It anchors the plant in the ground and absorbs nutrients and water from the soil.

Taproots are thick, tapering roots that grow downwards. Edible taproots include carrots, parsnips, and evening primrose. Many such plants have a biennial (two year) life cycle. In the first year, they form leafy rosettes. In the second year, a flowering stalk develops. Plants usually die after seeding. To avoid stunting their reproduction, biennial plants should only be collected in the rosette stage.

The following kinds of underground stems are storage organs for nutrients:

Rhizomes grow horizontally, store energy and colonize an area which gradually increases in size. As far as foraging, many wild rhizomes are very fibrous, although some are softer, and delicious.

Tubers are rhizomes that stop growing, become swollen, and store starchy nutrients. Examples are potato, wapato, and Jerusalem artichoke. Tubers are the plant's reproductive organs. New plants grow from their "eyes." Edible tubers are usually less fibrous than other types of roots.

Bulbs are modified stems with a papery covering. The leaves above the bulb carry out normal leaf functions. At the bottom of the bulb is a basal plate from which the roots grow. Well-known edible bulbs are onions and garlic. They store energy but are not reproductive organs.

Corms, similar to bulbs, are compressed stems. They have solid tissue rather than layers, however. Examples include water chestnuts, taro, and crocuses.

Nutritious and rich in carbohydrates, underground "vegetables" make tasty, filling meals. These plants are famine foods in some parts of the world.

Dig up underground stems or roots in late fall to early spring, when they will have the most flavor and nutrients. The leafy upper parts of the plant are dormant at these times of year. Be prepared to get your hands dirty for this kind of foraging, though. Collect minimally since harvesting often kills the plants.

SEASONAL SAVORING

You can forage all year, although edibles vary according to the seasons. For example, in regions with subzero winter temperatures, early spring is the time to harvest early wildflowers, hardy greens, new shoots, and underground stems or roots from dormant plants.

Many species become bitter and tough in warmer weather. As the season gains momentum, however, there are always plenty of greens, flowers, and shoots to pick during summer and early fall.

Spring delights include wild garlic or ramsons, lambsquarters, elder-flower blossoms, stinging nettles, ostrich fern fiddleheads, and wild mint.

As you'd expect, summer provides wild fruit, berries, wildflowers, and mild greens. Harvest summer species when they are completely ripe. Consume them quickly because of the heat.

In the fall, before the first hard frost, nature's bounty abounds. In addition to mild greens and fruits, your foraging may include nuts, seeds, roots, and bitter greens. Follow the example of squirrels to find white chestnuts, acorns, and pine nuts secreted in pinecones.

Even late fall and winter produce wild edibles for those willing to brave frigid temperatures to harvest dried fruits and berries, along with frost-hardy greens and roots.

KNOW YOUR PLANTS

In the next part of this book, you will finally meet 31 of the most common edible wild plants found across North America. Discover how to identify each plant, the habitat in which it grows, how to harvest it, cooking ideas, preparation tips, and even fun facts and trivia.

PART II
INTO THE WILD GREEN BEYOND

Forests are the lungs of the land.

— FRANKLIN D. ROOSEVELT

If you are reading the paperback version of this book and would like to access full-color versions of the photos, there is a QR code next to each photo in section 2. Just scan each code with your phone to see the color photo for each plant as you read about it.

Or to access the folder with photos of all 31 wild edible plants, scan this QR code or use the link below.

https://bit.ly/31EWPcolorphotos

AMARANTH

THE ANCIENT PROTEIN

AMARANTH

What's in a Name?

Plant Family: Amaranthaceae

Botanical and Common Names (Edible Species):

- *Amaranthus hypochondriacus* (prince's feather)
- *Amaranthus cruentus* (red amaranth)
- *Amaranthus caudatus* (love-lies-bleeding)

Amaranthus derives from the Greek word *amaranton*, which means "unfading," as the flowers retain their color and appearance for some time.

https://bit.ly/
amaranth_31EWP

Did You Know?

Amaranth has been grown for thousands of years. Cultivated by different peoples, including the Mayans and Incas, the Aztecs took it to a new level in the 1400s (Putman et al., 2022). They made offerings to the amaranth crop and used amaranth dough to sculpt effigies of their gods. When Spanish conquistadors outlawed the cultivation of this so-called sacred plant, local farmers secretly continued cultivating the seeds, even though the penalty was having their hands severed.

Amaranth is still used for cultural rituals and traditional recipes in Ethiopia and Southeast Asia. In Mexico, it is used for decorative calaveras (skulls) for the Day of the Dead festival.

Amaranth is a vivid plant, with stem and foliage colors ranging from bright pink to burgundy. Around 60–70 species occur worldwide (Petruzzello, n.d.). Particularly eye-catching varieties are grown as garden ornamentals. Amaranth readily colonizes vacant lots and wastelands. Only three species are edible, and several varieties are considered agricultural weeds. "Plainsman," an edible hybrid, is now cultivated in the United States as demand for amaranth health products increases.

Edible amaranths are delicious, high-protein plants originating in the Americas. They are simultaneously grain and seed, a "pseudocereal." The high-protein grain and tiny seeds can be milled into nutritious flour. Amaranth yields gluten-free grain, making it an ideal option for people who need to limit gluten in their diets. In Africa, amaranth is one of several plants known as "marog," where the leaves are eaten like spinach.

Plant Description

All edible amaranth species are tough, spreading annuals that grow from 3-8 feet tall (Putman et al., 2022). The stems, leaves, and taproot have some pinkish or maroon coloring. Stems are grooved lengthways and may have spines, maintaining thickness as they grow.

Leaves are large and simple, have smooth leaf margins, are arranged alternately on the stem, and are attached to it with a single stalk. Leaves are purplish or green and display distinctive patterns in some species.

Amaranth flowers may be green, purple, or golden. The tiny flowers form heavy, elongated clusters, usually at branch tips. They are arranged in showy spikes, plumes, or dense inflorescences (flower heads consisting of hundreds of tiny flowers).

Seeds of grain-bearing varieties are cream-colored, containing up to 3,000 seeds per gram (Department of Agriculture, Forestry and Fisheries, 2013).

Wholesome Goodness

Amaranth is extremely nutritious. The grain is 12%–17% protein and is high in fiber, with about 78% being insoluble (Putman et al., 2022). For people who don't eat much fiber, amaranth may take some time to get used to. Add it to your diet gradually, just to be on the safe side. Amaranth contains all nine amino acids essential for optimal health, as well as vitamins B and D, calcium, zinc, iron, magnesium, and phosphorus. It is low in saturated fat and may help lower cholesterol, thereby improving heart health. It could reduce inflammation and is rich in antioxidants.

Since ancient times, amaranth has been used to relieve anemia, upset stomach, and chronic fatigue syndrome, among other ailments.

Filling Your Basket

Both the leaves and seeds of amaranth are edible. You can gather individual leaves once they are the size of the palm of your hand. Larger leaves are best broken off the terminal growth tips of the stems.

Grain can be harvested once the plant is about six inches tall, usually at the end of summer. Some sources say it is best to harvest amaranth after the first frosts or a week of sunny weather to ensure the seeds are dry. The grain is ready to harvest when seeds are released as you gently shake the plumes.

Be careful not to lose the grain when harvesting. Harvest amaranth on a dry day after the morning dew has disappeared. Cut off the seed heads just before they become dry and brittle, and lay them on a clean tarp immediately. Alternatively, place them in paper bags with the heads down, and leave them in a shady spot to finish drying.

When the seed heads are dry, carefully remove them from the bag. Place a tray underneath the bag to catch any stray grain. Rub the seed head gently with your hands. It is best to wear gloves. If harvesting a larger quantity, lay the seed heads between two clean tarps and stamp on them with bare feet to loosen the seeds. Or smack two seed heads together over a cloth or large tray.

Once the dry seeds are removed, place them in a shallow bowl and swirl them around until the seed heads and chaff reach the surface. Tip the bowl to remove most of the chaff. You can then shake the seeds through a fine mesh screen. Winnowing them in a light breeze will also effectively remove the flower heads and chaff.

Forest to Table

Amaranth has an unusual flavor. Enthusiasts describe it as nutty, while others call it grassy, so you will have to form your own opinion.

Amaranth should be cooked before eating. Steam or boil the leaves like spinach. Simmer the seeds in water or stock, like rice or quinoa, adding chopped vegetables for variety, if desired. It cooks fairly quickly.

Use two and a half cups of water per cup of amaranth to make oatmeal-like porridge which you can eat with fruit and yogurt (Robbins, 2022).

Add the seeds to soups, stews, or homemade bread. You can grind amaranth grain into gluten-free flour. When baking with it, limit it to about a quarter of the amount required—the flour is heavy and makes baking very dense. Combine it with flours like almond, oat, or whole wheat, or use it as a thickener.

AMERICAN ELDERBERRY

THE IMMUNE-BOOSTER

What's in a Name?

Plant Family: Adoxaceae

Botanical Name: *Sambucus canadensis*

Common Names: American elder, American elderberry, common elderberry, black elderberry

Did You Know?

If you love exploring swamps, wandering beside trickling streams, or listening to mist drip from forest leaves, you'll probably come across the beautiful American elder. This large shrub bears dense clusters of tiny white flowers that attract summer butter-flies. Once the berries appear later in the season, birds and wildlife arrive for the feast.

https://bit.ly/
AmericanElderberry_31EWP

Although they have the potential to become invasive, American elders make attractive garden plants. Cultivated varieties are perfect for pollinators or rain gardens and help control soil erosion.

Indigenous Americans have used elders for centuries. The trees may have been cultivated in Europe as far back as 2,000 BCE (Health Hutt, 2019) and can still be found in old cottage gardens. According to English and Scandinavian folklore, an Elder Mother inhabited the tree.

Branches were hung in buildings for protection, and sprigs were placed on graves to facilitate the transition from life to death. The wood was used to make musical instruments for festivals and sacred feasts.

Elders are native to North America, Brazil, and Venezuela. While the American elder is native to North America, the black elder (S. nigra) is a European import. Another native elder is the blue or Mexican elder (S. cerulea), found west of the Rocky Mountains.

Besides moist locations, you might encounter elders on disturbed ground along roadsides, hedgerows, and recently burned areas.

Cautions

Always cook elderberries before eating.

Do not harvest or consume the elder shrub's roots, bark, stems, twigs, leaves, or seeds. All of these are toxic, containing a cyanide-producing glycoside.

If you find a similar herbaceous plant with whitish flowers or black berries, it is probably not an American elder. Be careful, because it might be a toxic look-alike.

Plant Description

American elders are deciduous (lose their leaves in winter), hardy, woody shrubs. They have a fibrous, shallow root system and grow in clumps, with individual canes reaching 9–12 feet (N.C. State Extension, n.d.).

The pinnately compound leaves are about five inches long and have 5–11 leaflets (Shmurak, 2020). They are opposite on the stem, occasionally attached by a very short leaf stalk. The leaves are long and serrated.

Flowers occur in flat, roundish clusters from 3–10 inches in diameter. They are yellowish-white and saucer-shaped, with five petals and five stamens (Shmurak, 2020). The flowers have a light, pleasant scent.

Fruits are rather inconspicuous berries that grow in large, drooping clusters. If the berries don't droop, you might be looking at the similar dwarf elder (S. ebulus). Sadly, its fruit is not edible and can actually make you very sick.

Black elderberries are dark purple to black, suspended on reddish stems. Blue elderberries are deep blue and often coated in whitish natural yeast, called "bloom". Red elders bear red, cone-shaped berries.

Look-Alike Plants

Poison hemlock flowers are often mistaken for elderflowers, although the resemblance is minimal. Poison hemlock shrubs are much smaller than elders. The blooms are true umbels, and plant stems have purple spots.

Pokeweed berries are much larger than elderberries and hang in a long cylinder. This plant is highly toxic, and the berries taste very unpleasant.

Devils walking stick is another plant that produces berries similar to the elder. However, the stem is covered with giant thorns.

Wholesome Goodness

Elderberries are incredibly nutritious, with twice as much vitamin C as oranges and three times the flavonoids of blueberries. They are brimming with antioxidants, which makes them a tremendous immune booster. In the Middle Ages, they were considered holy trees capable of restoring and maintaining good health. Hippocrates called elders "nature's medicine chest" (360 Farms, 2022). Elderflowers are rich in essential fatty acids. Flowers and berries may be used for culinary, medicinal, and cosmetic purposes.

The berries have been used traditionally for colds, flu, coughs, sore throats, anemia, insomnia, and anxiety. They are used in tonics and cough medications in North America and Europe.

Filling Your Basket

Elderflowers

Elderflowers peak from late spring to early summer, with some regional variation. Most people harvest the flowers in mid-June.

When harvesting elderflowers, look for white flowers that are fully open and have not started going brown. Never take more than 20%–30% of the flowers on any shrub, as they will eventually become berries to feed birds, wildlife, and people like you (Codekas, 2020). Use them fresh, dry them on a flower screen, or hang them on a rack to dry.

Elderberries

Elderberries are ready to harvest in August. However, they should only be harvested when completely ripe since green or partially ripe berries are toxic.

Forest to Table

Elderflowers have a delicate, sweet flavor similar to muscat grapes. Remember to remove the flowers from the stems. Eat the flowers fresh, sprinkled onto fruit salads, puddings, ice cream, or in punch. Use them in salads and stir-fries. Pickle the buds as a caper substitute.

Cook elderberries before eating to avoid unpleasant digestive effects. Mix them with grapes for jelly and add them to apples in pie filling. They also make delicious jam.

ARONIA BERRY

THE WILD SUPERFOOD

What's in a Name?

Plant Family: Rosaceae
Botanical Name: *Aronia arbutifolia*
Common Names: Aronia berry, chokeberry, red chokeberry

Aronia is derived from *aria*—the Greek name for the species *sorbus*, which bears similar-looking fruits. The genus name means "with leaves that are like Artibus." This is a genus of small trees and shrubs bearing edible fruit.

Did You Know?

The fruits of the black aronia berry were traditionally used by Indigenous Americans to relieve colds, flu, and related ailments. In the first half of the 20th century, these berries were introduced to Russia and Europe for the fruit industry.

Aronia berries are multi-stemmed deciduous shrubs. Different parts can be used in every season. The berries attract the most interest but have a tart, bitter-sweet taste, hence one of the common names, chokeberry. There are three types: red, purple, and black aronia berries, with the red variety being the sweetest and most palatable. The

https://bit.ly/ AroniaBerry_31EWP

berries make thick jam because they contain pectin, the substance used to thicken jam and jelly. Aronia berries are rich in nutrients. The shrubs are attractive and are planted in pollinator and winter gardens. Their flowers can also be harvested and used.

Aronia berries form thickets or colonies in the wild, as they spread via stem suckers. They occur in eastern Canada, in the central U.S., and along the eastern seaboard. The plants like water and you will find them in moist woods, swamps, and the margins of lakes. They blossom in spring and bear berries in fall.

Foraging Tip: Look for the flowering shrubs in spring, note their location, and return to harvest the berries in fall.

Plant Description

These shrubs have a vase-like shape and reach a height of between 6 and 10 feet (N.C. Extension, n.d.). They grow rigidly upright and have a fibrous root system.

Leaves are oval, with finely toothed edges, and are up to three inches long (Pesaturo, 2014). They are arranged alternately on plant stems.

The back of the leaf is paler than the upper side. The particular species can be identified by looking at the underside of the leaves. Red and purple aronia leaves have a wooly appearance, while black aronia leaves are virtually smooth.

Flowers appear in late spring after the late frosts. Each flower has five white, roundish petals, and about 20 stamens ranging from pale pink to deep purple (Pesaturo, 2014). As many as 30 flowers make up a two-inch diameter cluster (University of Maine, n.d.).

Berries are small, a third to half an inch in diameter. Black aronia berries are glossy and black when ripe. They hang down in clusters from red pedicels (fruit stalks). There may be anything from 3–30 fruits in each. The fruits are like tiny apples with 3–5 seeds (University of Maine, n.d.).

Look-Alike Plants

The bitter berry or Virginia bird cherry may be confused with aronia berries. These are considered pests because they host caterpillars that damage the fruit. The stone of bitter berry fruit is poisonous to wild and domestic ruminant animals. Since there is cyanide in its leaves, consumption of the leaves by animals and humans can be fatal.

Wholesome Goodness

Aronia berries are considered a superfood because they contain more antioxidants than any other berry. They also contain zinc, magnesium, iron, and vitamins B, C, and K.

Adding these berries to your diet can help manage diabetes, positively influencing insulin levels. Aronia berries are also helpful for inflammation and can boost immunity.

Filling Your Basket

The berries ripen in fall, from mid-August to September, depending on the species and location. Harvest them as soon as they ripen, because the fruits quickly shrivel up and drop off the plants. You can simply pick berries off the plants or use a berry rake to make harvesting easier.

Forest to Table

Because the berries are very astringent, it is recommended that you add sugar or another sweetener and use them for jams and jellies. The berries can also be cooked and strained to make juice since cooking reduces their tartness. Berries can be frozen for later use.

ARROWHEAD

THE POTATO FOR DUCKS

What's in a Name?

Plant Family: Alismataceae

Botanical Name: *Sagittaria latifolia*

Common Names: Broadleaf arrowhead, duck potato, Indian potato, wapato, katniss

Did You Know?

If you don't mind wet feet and getting muddy, you will enjoy foraging for these tasty tubers. Arrowhead derives its common name from their distinctive arrowhead-shaped leaves. They are native to North America, where there are 24 species (Stephenson, 2021). One of the most common is the broadleaf arrowhead (Sagittaria latifolia). Their edible, tuberous roots grow in the slimy mud bordering ponds, lakes, and marshes, although their leaves grow several feet above the water.

https://bit.ly/ ArrowheadFlower_31EWP

Broadleaf arrowhead originated in southern Canada. It has now spread throughout the United States and to Central and South America, Europe, and Southeast Asia.

Arrowhead is a deciduous plant and thrives in sunny locations. It colonizes the shallows of freshwater wetlands, including ponds, lakes, the edges of ditches, and swamps.

https://bit.ly/ ArrowheadTuber_31EWP

Plant Description

Arrowhead plants usually grow 4–6.5 feet tall (although they can reach heights of 65 feet) (Health Benefits Times, 2016). They have tough, fibrous roots with long, spreading stolons that bear the tubers.

Leaves grow in a rosette, rising vertically. They have long, triangular, spongy leaf stalks. The blades are sagittate or arrowhead-shaped, and relatively large, about 12 inches long and 6 inches wide (Health Benefits Times, 2016). There is considerable variation in leaf length and width, however. The upper leaf surface is greener than the underside. Leaves immersed in water have no leaf blades.

Flowers are white, bearing three rounded petals arranged in whorls of three. Flower stalks are 8–16.5 inches long; each bears 2–8 whorls of flowers. Petals are small, usually under an inch in length. Male flowers have over 20 bushy yellow stamens in the center, while female flowers have a green central mound (Health Benefits Times, 2016). Flowers have small boat-shaped bracts.

Roots are white or bluish, tough and fibrous, with long, spreading stolons. The latter are thin and white, producing white tubers covered with translucent, purplish skin, about the size of chicken eggs.

Look-Alike Plants

The poisonous arrow arum looks similar but can easily be distinguished by the number of leaf veins. If there are only three, you have found the toxic arum. If there are several leaf veins, you are looking at arrowhead, which is safe to eat.

Wholesome Goodness

Early European explorers Lewis and Clark crossed North America, reaching the Pacific Ocean on November 15, 1805. Afterward, they built a stockade named Fort Clatsop, where "Indian potatoes" sustained them throughout the winter (Fertig, n.d.). That's not surprising, because arrowhead tubers are an excellent source of carbohydrates, essential vitamins, and minerals. One hundred grams of arrowroot tubers will provide 881 mg of potassium, 197 mg of phosphorus, and 16.14 g of carbs (Health Benefits Times, 2016). In addition, the plants contain vitamins B1 and B6, magnesium, iron, and copper.

Indigenous Americans used leaf poultices to stop milk production. They treated wounds and sores with root poultices, while arrowhead leaf tea was one of their natural headache remedies.

Filling Your Basket

Arrowhead tubers, seedpods, leaves, and stalks are all edible, but young leaves and stalks are the most tender during spring and early summer. Flowers bloom from July to August. The seedpods can be eaten in fall, also the season that tubers are ripe and ready to harvest.

Cut the leaves, stalks, and seedpods off the plant using a sharp knife. Harvest the furled leaves and take flower stalks before the flower opens. Be careful not to take too many leaves, as the plant needs them to produce food for itself. Harvest small amounts from several plants and never take more than you need.

If you've ever dug up potatoes, you will be delighted to know that arrowhead tubers are comparatively easy to harvest. Simply wade into the shallow water and find them with your feet. Reach down and pull them up or loosen them from the roots. You can also use a stick or pitchfork but be careful not to cut the tubers with the prongs. The tubers float around on the surface once freed and can be collected effortlessly.

Forest to Table

Arrowhead tubers taste like potatoes or chestnuts and can be prepared similarly. Peel off the outer skin before boiling or baking the tubers. They taste better peeled, although the skin is edible, so try it if you want.

Flower stalks and leaves should be boiled before eating. Roasting is another cooking option for the leaves.

BASSWOOD

THE FRAGRANT LINDEN TREE

What's in a Name?
Plant Family: Tiliaceae
Botanical Name: *Tilia americana*
Common Names: Basswood tree, American basswood, American
linden, lime tree

The basswood tree was used by most Indigenous Americans for fiber
rather than food. Bass is a corruption of the English word "bast", a
type of fiber. The bark was soaked for two to four weeks to loosen the
long fibers, which were used for everything from basket-making to
sewing thread and wound sutures (Deane, 2018).

The basswood tree is the only representative of its genus in the entire Western Hemisphere, although there are local varieties. Basswood trees are also known as linden trees.

https://bit.ly/
Basswood_31EWP

Did You Know?

If you go to the woods in the summertime, you might catch the sweet, gentle scent of basswood trees in full bloom, in clearings or at the edge of woodlands. Their white flower clusters fill the air with a fragrance faintly reminiscent of honey.

The linden tree is Aphrodite's sacred tree, according to Greek mythology. In Germany, the Elf King supposedly lived beneath a linden tree that attracted dwarves and dragons and put heroes into an enchanted sleep. Judicial meetings and trials were conducted beneath basswood trees, which were credited with the ability to encourage truthfulness.

Basswood is native to northeastern North America. It produces light wood used for furniture and utensils. The leaves and seeds are edible, while the sap may be made into a sweet syrup.

Although the trees bloom only briefly, the sweet-smelling flowers attract masses of bees which produce unusual, delicious honey. Butterfly and moth caterpillars eat basswood leaves. Chipmunks, mice, and squirrels eat the seeds, while voles and rabbits eat the bark. Both leaves and seeds are safe for human consumption.

Plant Description

The American basswood is a deciduous tree that reaches an average height of 60–120 feet, although it occasionally grows as tall as 128 feet. It grows faster than most North American hardwoods and may live for as long as 200 years (Wikipedia, 2020).

BASSWOOD

It is usually found in mixed upland forests and rarely forms colonies. It tolerates flooding so well that it sometimes grows on floodplains.

Young trees have cone-shaped canopies that become round over time. Basswoods sprout from the base and do not rely exclusively on seeds for reproduction. There are often several tall trees around the base of the original tree. It has a shallow root system with laterally spreading roots. Branches are small, weak, and drooping.

Leaves are simple, alternately arranged on the stem, and about 4–6 inches in size, although they may reach 10 inches (Wikipedia, 2020). They are long, tapering, and heart-shaped with explicitly toothed margins. They are attached to the branches by long slender leaf stalks. Leaves begin falling in September.

Flowers are white and light green, found in clusters dangling from a long stalk attached to a papery bract. On average, a cluster contains between six and twenty flowers. Each flower has five cream-colored petals and sepals. Stamens are grouped into five clusters, the anthers turning brown when mature (Wikipedia, 2020).

Fruits are gray-green nutlets covered in fine, gray hairs and containing one seed each. They are formed after the flower has been fertilized. Nutlets begin dropping to the ground in early fall, but the tree may continue releasing them, sometimes for years. The bract catches the breeze and carries the seeds away from the tree.

Look-Alike Plants

Backyard linden, boulevard linden, Dakota linden, pyramidal linden, and redmond linden are cultivated varieties of basswood.

Wholesome Goodness

The leaves contain vitamins and minerals, while the bark yields starchy carbohydrates. Basswood flowers are used in cosmetic products, mainly in Europe. They include antioxidant flavonoids, volatile oils, and mucilaginous constituents that reduce inflammation. The flowers also contain tannins that have an astringent action.

Brew a pleasant-tasting flower tea to relieve colds, coughs, and headaches. Basswood flower tea also induces sleep.

Filling Your Basket

Basswood trees are a natural fast food. The tiny young leaves are the most palatable when they are light green and shiny, making tasty "forest greens." Harvest them in spring by pinching them off the branches. Once they are about half the size of full-grown leaves, they become tough.

You can also eat new spring shoots. Harvest them sparingly, though, as these are young trees starting to grow.

Basswoods bear prolific, sweet flowers from April to July. Pick buds and flowers straight from the tree and eat them immediately. They are best eaten raw. The nutlets are another tasty and nutritious natural snack. They start falling from the tree in October and can be collected from the ground.

The trees produce sweet sap that runs down the trunk in spring, just before the leaves open. This can be harvested to make syrup.

Forest to Table

Eat young, new leaves raw or use them in salads, like lettuce. You can cook them instead, but this reduces both flavor and bulk. Leaf buds are just as tasty as the leaves. Eat them immediately after picking or pinching off the tree.

In spring, you can harvest the cambium, the tissue between the outer bark and the wood. Its flavor is reminiscent of a slightly sweet cucumber. Add fresh cambium to soups or dry it and grind it into powder for homemade bread and savory dishes.

You can make tea from the flower. Use two teaspoons per cup, allowing it to steep until the delectable flavor infuses the drink (Monteanu, 2021). The flowers can be dried, but to avoid reducing their flavor and nutritional properties, don't dry flowers in the oven.

The nutlets, as mentioned previously, can be harvested from the ground and eaten raw. Discard the green outer sheath and pop the seed into your mouth. You won't need to buy trail mix with excellent wilderness food like this.

Chocoholics might like to try making basswood chocolate. In the 18th century, a French chemist found that he could produce a choco-late-flavored paste by combining dried linden flowers with unripe nutlets (Monteanu, 2021). Some foragers still do this today.

BLACK LOCUST

THE FEATHERY HARDWOOD

What's in a Name?

Family Name: Fabaceae

Botanical Name: *Robinia pseudoacacia*

Common Names: Black locust, yellow locust, brown locust, false acacia

The Latin word *locusta*, which means both "locust" and "lobster," is the reason that this tree has been known as the black locust tree since the 1640s (Wikipedia, 2021).

Did You Know?

From a distance, black locust trees have an oddly feathery appearance because of the abundant leaflets they bear. Your nose will lead you to them in the summer, as the edible flowers emit a heady

https://bit.ly/BlackLocust1-31EWP

aroma, similar to mock oranges and reminiscent of peach jelly. They have several health benefits too.

Also called false acacia, black locust trees are native to the eastern United States. While they occur in several types of forests, they grow best in the Appalachian Mountains, where they originated. Botanists believe that black locust trees were exported by Indigenous Americans from the mountains to the coast. When Europeans arrived, the trees were already established around traditional homesteads. The wood was used to make bows.

Black locust trees are hardy, competitive plants, surviving deep droughts and harsh winters. These trees reproduce by sending up root suckers from the stump, thereby creating numerous clones connected by a fibrous root system. While this has advantages— black locusts are often planted to stop soil erosion—it also makes the trees very invasive. However, locust leaf miners and locust borers attack them. The borer tunnels into the bark, weakening the trees, which may collapse in high winds.

The wood is incredibly hard and strong. During the gold rush, the trees were brought to California, where their timber was used to shore up mine workings. The trees were subsequently planted there to supply railroad timber. Black locust wood was also used to construct the first buildings and for the colonial gardens in Jamestown. They were trendy ornamental trees in the 1800s in both England and America.

In the war of 1812 in Lake Champlain, the American fleet had a decisive victory at Plattsburg Bay. (Greene, 2015). Part of the reason for this, it was believed, was because the American ships were built using locust nails. Facing cannon fire, the American ships held together, whereas the British ships broke apart. The day the war ended, the British began importing locust nails by the tens of thousands, a trade that continues today.

Cautions

The trees are toxic if eaten by livestock, especially horses, and fatalities are likely.

Also poisonous to people, the leaves, twigs, bark, and seeds must not be eaten or used medicinally or in any other way.

Plant Description

The black locust is a large, perennial, deciduous tree. It grows extremely fast, to over 10 feet, although trees as high as 50 feet have been recorded. It rarely survives 100 years, however (Austin, 2005). The bark is gray, thickly furrowed, and so distinctive that you will probably be able to identify the black locust from its bark alone. The twigs are thin, sometimes with small thorns on the ends. The trunks of young trees often bear thorns as well.

Leaves have smooth margins and are attached to the stem with leaf stalks (Austin, 2005; Unruly Gardening, 2022). Leaves are pinnately compound and arranged alternately on the stem. Each leaf comprises 7–20 leaflets. The leaflets are oval, rounded, and slightly pointed at the ends. Each one is about 0.5–2 inches long. At night, the leaflets fold up and droop.

Flowers resemble those of garden peas. They are white with a pinkish base and grow in drooping clusters 6–8 inches long (Unruly Gardening, 2022). The flowers dangle from the thin twigs and blow in the wind.

Fruits are long, green pods that turn brown and dry when the seeds are ready for release.

Wholesome Goodness

The flowers contain a chemical believed to shrink tumors. Cooked flowers can be used to relieve eye problems. To treat burns, apply crushed flowers to the affected skin for a few hours. An infusion is helpful for digestive ailments.

Filling Your Basket

The flowers are the only part of this tree that is edible. The tree flowers in spring, usually in late April or early May. They are ready to harvest when a yellow spot appears on the flowers.

You can pick the flowers off the tree one at a time, but it's easier to run your hand along the cluster, pulling off several flowers simultaneously. If you harvest this way, carefully pick out any leaves that may have gotten mixed in with the blooms.

Forest to Table

Black locust flowers are slightly crunchy and taste like sweet spring peas. Use them fresh off the tree, as they deteriorate quickly. Eat them raw as a natural snack or add them to salads. Unless you want extra protein, make sure you examine the flowers carefully for bugs. Avoid washing the flowers, as this reduces their scent and flavor. You can also make flower tea jelly. The flowers last a month or two if stored in the freezer.

BLACKBERRY

THE THORNIEST SHRUB TO LOVE

What's in a Name?

Plant Family: Rosaceae
Botanical Name:

- *Rubus fruticosus*
- *Rubus ursinus*
- *Rubus allegheniensis*
- *Rubus canadensis*
- *Rubus arcticus*

Common Names: Blackberry

There are over 375 species of wild blackberries which grow north of the equator and even in South America. Several of the most common North American species are listed above.

https://bit.ly/ Blackberries_31EWP

Other berries in the genus *Rubus* include raspberries, dewberries, tayberries, loganberries, boysenberries, youngberries, marionberries, and salmonberries. All yield tasty fruit.

BLACKBERRY

Did You Know?

No one knows quite where blackberries originated, although people have eaten them since ancient times, and they were included in festival foods. Iron Age peoples ate them, the Romans used them medicinally, and Indigenous Americans obtained food, medicine, and dye from them. Over 2,000 years ago, Europeans used blackberries for fruit, medicine, and hedgerows (Grant, 2018). The canes were used for weaving baskets, thatching roofs, and making bee hives. In Devon, England, stems were used to make fishing rods and pull rabbits from burrows. Today, Mexico is the world's top blackberry producer, while the U.S. ranks third in global raspberry production (FoodPrint, 2022).

Blackberries abound in midsummer. The ripe berries are perfect for eating fresh or adding to fruit salads and desserts. You can also make jams and jellies to enjoy after the season ends. The bounty comes at a price, however. Even more plentiful than blackberry fruits are their thorns, which will catch on your clothing, scratch your arms, and entangle your hair.

While you'll probably focus on the berries, remember that the leaves and stems are also edible.

Plant Description

Blackberries have many forms. Most are loose shrubs, while others trail like ground-hugging vines. The bushes are rarely taller than five feet (Everett, 2021). The stems are tangled and thorny with different degrees of prickliness.

Leaves are compound, comprising 3–5 leaflets, although there are occasionally other forms (Everett, 2021). They bear small thorns and have toothed leaf margins. The leaves turn reddish-purple in fall.

Flowers are reminiscent of roses with five petals (Everett, 2021). Flower colors differ depending on the species.

Berries are actually clusters of tiny single fruits combined. They come off the bush along with the receptacle. In this they differ from raspberries, which pop off the receptacle like a small cup. The fruits are initially green but later turn red and then ripen to a lovely shade of purplish-black.

Look-Alike Plants

The invasive multiflora rose looks similar to blackberry bushes, even down to the thorns. This look-alike has leaves with seven leaflets connected by leafy tissue rather than leaf stalks. While they flower at the same time of year as blackberries, the roses bear flowers in much heavier, denser clusters. Although the multiflora roses won't yield berries, you can harvest its tiny rose hips in mid-fall.

Wholesome Goodness

Blackberries are deliciously nutritious, a true superfood. One cup contains half the recommended daily dose of vitamin C (FoodPrint, 2022). In addition, blackberries have a significant amount of calcium, potassium, vitamin C, phosphorus, magnesium, and fiber. They are also impressively rich in antioxidants and anthocyanins.

For centuries, blackberry cordial or wine has been used to revitalize ill or convalescing people. Leaves, roots, and shoots have relieved numerous common ailments, while blackberry vinegar was taken for colds, gout, and arthritis.

If you keep bees, they love the blossoms and will make tasty honey from their nectar.

Filling Your Basket

Leaves and Stems

Deterred by the thorns, most foragers rarely consider blackberry leaves and stems. You can, however, harvest young leaves and new stems in early spring when the foliage is tender and the thorns are minimal or very soft.

Berries

Pick berries from midsummer to early fall, when they are deep red or intense blue-black, depending on the variety. Pick them directly from the bush. The sweetest ones will practically fall into your hands.

Forest to Table

Use young leaves in salads and sauté them like spinach. Steam tender stems and eat them as a vegetable or add them to omelets, stir-fries, and similar dishes. Use the fruit to make jams, jellies, cordials, pie fillings, chutneys, ketchup, or flavored vinegar.

BURDOCK

THE TENACIOUS EURASIAN ONE

What's in a Name?

Plant Family: Asteraceae

Botanical Name: *Arctium lappa, Arctium minus*

Common Names: Common burdock, lesser burdock, giant burdock, bardane

Arctium is derived from the Greek word *arktos*, meaning "bear", possibly a reference to the toughness of the plant's enormous, seed-bearing burrs, which attach themselves to nearly everything. "Dock" refers to the plant's large leaves.

Did You Know?

Indigenous Americans depended on burdock for nourishment and medicine. They boiled the roots in maple syrup for a sweet treat and stored them during winter.

Swiss inventor George de Mestral conceived the idea for Velcro when removing the burrs from his dog's coat. NASA used it for spacesuits; thus, in Margaret Roberts's words, "burdock became the first wild plant in space" (Roberts, 2012).

https://bit.ly/
Burdock_31EWP

Burdock is a wildflower that originated in Eurasia and now grows throughout North America, except in the south. Depending on your viewpoint, it is either a weedy invasive or hardy survivor, found in open land almost anywhere. Burdock is hard to eradicate as it has a deep taproot and produces copious seeds (15,000 per plant) that remain viable for years (N.C. Extension, n.d.). However, bees feast on the flowers and make delectable honey from the nectar. Burdock also provides food for painted lady butterfly caterpillars.

Once considered a crucial edible plant, burdock has been largely forgotten, although it is still harvested in Asia. Find this enormous plant in sunny places on waste ground, along roadsides and footpaths, on the edges of farm fields, and in vacant lots. The entire plant is edible, including its huge leaves and towering flower stem. Burdock is an important medicinal plant.

Plant Description

Burdock is an herbaceous, biennial wildflower that grows to a height of 3–6 feet, facilitated by its deep taproot (Stephenson, 2021). The plant grows leaves in the first year, sending up a very long flowering stem that bears thistle-like flowers in its second year.

Leaves are enormous, wavy, and heart-shaped. They are green above and pale underneath. They create a massive ground-hugging rosette that may reach three feet in diameter (Roberts, 2012).

Flowers grow from a long five-foot-high stalk that shoots up when the plant has been growing for about 18 months (Roberts, 2012). Purple flowers form on the tips of a prickly ball of bracts. Flowerheads are ⅓–1 inch wide and composed of purple disc florets surrounded by several rows of overlapping, hooked bracts (Stephenson, 2021). They look somewhat like thistles.

Seeds form large burrs that disperse themselves by hooking onto clothing, animal hides, and fur.

Look-Alike Plants

Common burdock may be confused with the wooly or downy burdock. However, the wooly burdock has distinctive cobwebby hairs on the flower bracts. While it is edible, it is much more bitter than common burdock.

Wholesome Goodness

Burdock could be classified as a superfood. It contains significant dietary fiber and numerous antioxidants and is excellent for fighting inflammation and building immunity. Its roots contain potassium, folate, phosphorus, calcium, iron, and vitamins B6 and C.

The plant's primary uses are detoxifying and cleansing. It is also antiseptic and mildly antibiotic. The roots help to remove and eliminate heavy metals from the blood. It was once grown near coal mines and polluted areas, and workers took burdock tea to remove toxins from their bodies.

Filling Your Basket

Harvest young plant stems in early spring before they become hard and bitter. This is also the best time to forage the new, tender leaves.

The root is the best part of the plant to harvest, however. Do this in the spring or fall of the plant's second year before it becomes fibrous and woody. Getting burdock roots out of the ground is challenging due to this plant's persistence in colonizing inhospitable spots.

Forest to Table

Eat first-year roots and second-year stems like a vegetable but cook them first for about 20 minutes (Stephenson, 2021). Peel and scrub burdock stems before cooking to remove the bitter outer sheath. Eat immature flower stalks in late spring before flowers appear. They taste a bit like artichokes. Boil and then stir-fry them for an unusual vegetable treat.

The root tastes like a cross between a chestnut and a parsnip. In Japan, it is called *gobo*, and used in many traditional dishes. Cook the taproot any way you wish, from roasting to frying. You can even use it to make a coffee substitute.

CATTAIL

THE CAT THAT LIKES WATER

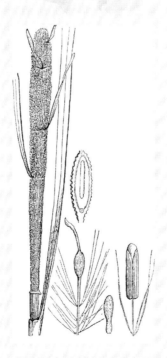

What's in a Name?

Plant Family: Typhaceae

Botanical Name: *Typha latifolia*

Common Names: Common cattail, broadleaf cattail, cat-o-nine-tails, reeds, bulrush, Cossack asparagus

These plants get their names from the fuzzy, elongated seed heads that remind some people of cats and their tails.

Did You Know?

Archaeological evidence suggests that cattail rhizomes may have been eaten in Europe as far back as 30,000 years ago (Wikipedia, 2020). Indigenous Americans ate the rhizomes, young stems, and flowers. The leaves were woven into matting and baskets, while the soft down from ripening seed heads was used for padding.

https://bit.ly/Cattail_31EWP

While native to North America, cattails, or bulrushes as often called in other countries, grow in many regions of the world. Cattails are so prolific that it's hard to overharvest them. The shoots are easy to collect, while the rhizomes are a little more complicated. Oh, and just as a friendly warning, you'll probably get soaked and encounter lots of mosquitoes.

This plant loves having wet feet, and it's always associated with water. It grows at higher elevations (4,200–9,600 feet) and is found in all freshwater aquatic habitats, from irrigation canals to dam backwaters. It won't, however, grow in areas where the water is deeper than 5.6 feet (Utah State University, n.d.).

Although this plant often grows near reeds, it is considered a perennial herb. It has a very erect growth habit. Strut-like structures inside the leaves give the plants rigidity, enabling them to stand tall.

Cattails are prolific plants. Each fluffy seed head produces as many as 280,000 seeds (Utah State University, n.d.). The plants also reproduce vegetatively through the rhizomes, a single rhizome producing as many as 100 new stalks in one growing season (National Park Service, 2018).

Cautions

Sensitive individuals may experience stomach upsets and loss of appetite when eating cattails or using any parts of the plant medicinally. Start off by eating minimal amounts and see how your body reacts.

Cattails are used in Africa during childbirth because of their hormone-like compounds that stimulate the uterus and cause contractions. Pregnant and breastfeeding women should not eat any plant parts whatsoever or use them medicinally.

These plants also contain compounds that thin the blood. Do not eat cattails or use them medicinally if you are on blood-thinning medication, as this could increase the effects.

Plant Description

Cattails grow in dense clumps and reach heights of 4–8 feet (TWC Staff, 2019). These evergreen plants are aquatic or semi-aquatic and prefer locations with full sun to partial shade. Their stiff, unbranched stems grow from 3–10 feet tall. The root consists of numerous tough rhizomes 3–4 inches below the soil surface. These may grow up to 27 inches in length with a diameter of 0.2–1.2 inches (Utah State University, n.d.). Cattails reproduce via both the rhizomes and seeds.

Leaves originate from the base of the plant and are narrow, upright, and sword-shaped. Each plant bears 12–16 thin leaves that may be as long as seven feet (Utah State University, n.d.).

Flowers are borne on a flower stalk topped by two sets of minute flowers tightly packed into a cylindrical inflorescence (Utah State University, n.d.). The yellowish male flowers are located at the top, with the greenish female flowers below. The flowers bloom in summer, and afterward, the male flowers rapidly disperse, leaving the stalk naked.

Seeds emanate from pollinated female flowers, which brown as the seeds mature, forming sausage-like fruiting spikes up to 9 inches long (Utah State University, n.d.).

Fruits have bristly hairs and are released when the spike bursts during dry weather. The wind blows the fruit to new locations, where they accumulate in dense mats. When they come into contact with water, the seed is released.

Look-Alike Plants

Cattails may be confused with common reeds and bulrushes.

Wholesome Goodness

Cattails are an excellent source of nutrients. They contain significant amounts of manganese, as well as magnesium, calcium, iron, sodium, vitamin K, and some dietary fiber (Firdous, 2020). They are also high in carbohydrates.

Cattails have natural antiseptic properties. A gel found between young leaves can be used to treat wounds and prevent infection. In addition, it is a powerful painkiller. Cattail extract promotes blood clotting and helps stop bleeding.

Filling Your Basket

Foraging Tip: Before harvesting cattails, ensure the surrounding water is clean and free of contaminants such as chemicals, animal manure, and trash.

Cut young shoots off the rhizomes in spring and summer when they are between 14–16 inches tall (Tesolin, 2022). Or you can take the entire plant. They become more fibrous as the season progresses, so forage early for the best taste experience.

First, look for the unique brown fruit, fuzzy seed heads, and slightly mottled brown and cream tops to ensure that you are harvesting the right plant. Then, find a cattail about the size of a broom handle at the base. With a firm grip just above the waterline, use both hands to wriggle it until it loosens so you can pull it out. The shoots should be large and white. Place the entire plant in a plastic garbage bag to take home. Cattail shoots are best eaten immediately.

Collect the pollen to use as flour. Collect it when the plants are slightly green and just starting to brown. Find one that's beginning to show a fuzzy yellow bit above the tail. Gently bend the cattail and place it inside a large jar or container. Then shake it to release the pollen into the jar. You should get about a tablespoon of pollen per cattail (Tesolin, 2022).

You can also eat the rhizomes, which are best harvested in fall and winter. They are high in starch with some protein included.

Forest to Table

Cut off the rhizome (if you have harvested it) and remove the outer husk, which separates easily. Peel off the layers until you get to the center core and separate the rest of the plant from the white, tender shoot. Eat them raw—they taste like cucumber. If you steam them, they taste like cauliflower. You can also pickle them.

Remove the outer sheath and steam or boil the stalks or flowerheads, as you would corn-on-the-cob. The gelatinous substance in the leaves can be used to thicken soups and stews. Add the pollen to bread, pancakes, and even pasta.

Rhizomes have a relatively sweet flavor. Cook them like potatoes and include the lower part of the stem. They can be baked, roasted, boiled—or even eaten raw. The inner rhizome can be dried and ground to make flour.

CHICKWEED

THE LITTLE SPRING STAR

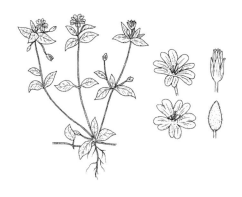

What's in a Name?

Plant Family: Caryophyllaceae

Botanical Name: *Stellaria media*

Common Names: Chickweed, starweed, scarwort, stitch weed, winter weed, birdweed

Stellaria means "star" and describes the shape of chickweed flowers. *Media* means "in the midst of." This nutritious plant is often fed to poultry, which explains its common name.

https://bit.ly/ Chickweed_31EWP

Did You Know?

If you've joined the craze for eating weeds, then you've likely discovered chickweed. Originally native to Europe, chickweed now grows worldwide and was introduced to North America by immigrants, who used it as an herb. It can be used as a famine food because it grows during winter.

CHICKWEED

Common chickweed is a winter annual in temperate regions, but it may also be a biennial or a short-lived perennial. Seeds germinate in fall, with plants growing in spring and summer. Chickweed invades plots and agricultural grain lands. It prefers shady, moist locations, and appears opportunistically in favorable conditions, including in gardens, so you might find this edible wild plant without leaving home. Much to the dismay of gardeners but to the delight of foragers, chickweed seeds prolifically. One plant can produce an impressive 30,000 seeds that remain viable for up to 30 years (Chandran, 2020).

Plant Description

Chickweed is a mat-forming plant that grows up to 12 inches tall (Media and Vill, 2006). Stems are light green and hairy, usually running along the ground, rooting at the nodes. Only the upper portion of the stem is erect, branching freely as it grows. The root system is shallow and fibrous. Plants live for about six weeks (Khron, 2021).

Leaves are bright green, opposite, and occur in pairs at regular intervals on plant stems. They change positions at each node, forming a cross pattern.

Flowers are tiny and star-like, giving the impression of having ten petals, although they actually have only five rabbit-shaped petals (Krohn, 2021). The flowers stay open for about 12 hours in full sun but remain closed in overcast weather. Plants bloom sporadically for about 1–2 months (N.C. Extension, n.d.). Seeds are enclosed in a drooping, hairy capsule.

Wholesome Goodness

Compared to spinach, chickweed has 12 times more calcium, 5 times more magnesium, 85 times more iron, and 6 times more vitamin C (Khron, 2021). It is high in antioxidants, B vitamins, and zinc, a natural immune booster. In addition, chickweed contains saponins, which increase the body's ability to absorb nutrients and act as natural appetite suppressants.

Because of this plant's soothing, cooling, hydrating, and healing properties, it is used as a tea or poultice for numerous ailments and medical conditions.

Filling Your Basket

Chickweed loves cool, damp spring weather and grows well through March and April. Harvest the tender new growth with scissors or cut the tops off more established plants. Rinse to remove any dirt. Chickweed will keep in the refrigerator for several days if placed in a paper towel or plastic bag.

After seeding, the plants become fibrous and unpalatable. Wait for the next batch to harvest them again.

Forest to Table

Chickweed has a pleasant, mild flavor when harvested young. You can eat both the leaves and flowers raw or cooked. Toss them into salads, stir-fries, stews, pesto, scrambled eggs, or lasagna. Boil the leaves as potherbs. You can dry chickweed for adding to soups, breads, and sauces.

CHICORY

THE PRETTY BLUE DANDELION

What's in a Name?

Plant Family: Asteraceae

Botanical Name: *Cichorium intybus*

Common Names: Chicory, blue daisy, blue dandelion, blue weed, coffee weed

Did You Know?

The closest contact most people have with chicory is instant coffee, as many manufacturers use chicory to give the beverage its distinctive taste. Until they produce their lovely purplish-blue flowers, chicory plants resemble dandelions in the field. And there are many uses for this plant.

https://bit.ly/ Chicory_3IEWP

Hailing from the Mediterranean, chicory was initially used for salads and as a coffee substitute. The Romans saw the medicinal benefits of chicory and cultivated a robust variety not available today. From the

1700s until the 1950s, chicory was grown on farms and homesteads throughout North America (Dodrill, 2022).

This plant is extremely bitter. Its roots are used medicinally and to make a caffeine-free coffee substitute. Plants grow in sunny places such as roadside ditches, waste ground, abandoned fields, and farmyards. Chicory is a low-growing plant resembling a dandelion or wild lettuce, so make sure of your identification before picking, although all three of these plants are edible. You can eat the entire chicory plant, including its leaves, flowers, and roots.

Plant Description

Chicory is a perennial that grows as a leafy rosette before sending up a sturdy, leafless stem with a hairy base. In the rosette stage, it closely resembles a dandelion. However, the chicory flower stalk has only small, sparsely distributed leaves. It is about 2–5 feet tall with several thin branches and is filled with milky sap (Dodrill, 2022). Wild chicory has a long taproot that is darker than a dandelion root.

Leaves are large, lobed, and hairy, forming a rosette at the base of the plant. The lower leaves have deep lobes and are lace-like, with the lobes reducing towards the end of the leaf. The ground leaves are about 3–6 inches long (Dodrill, 2022). Young leaves are egg-shaped, slightly shiny, and pale green. The leaves decrease in size further up the stem.

Flowers are easily identified. The stems bear relatively unscented, purplish-blue flowers that resemble asters. Chicory flowers are about 1.5 inches in diameter and can have as many as 20 petals on one head (Dodrill, 2022). Each petal has a fringe-like structure on the broad end. The flowers open and close during the day, opening mainly in the mornings.

Seeds are flat and oblong, measuring about half an inch long. Each plant produces around 3,000 seeds (Dodrill, 2022).

Look-Alike Plants

Edible plants resembling chicory include dandelion, cat's ear, Japanese hawkwood, salsify, sow thistle, and wild lettuce. They can be distinguished primarily by subtle differences in the leaves.

Wholesome Goodness

Chicory is high in calcium, manganese, zinc, sodium, folic acid, iron, potassium, and vitamins A, B6, C, E, and K.

Oligofructose derived from the inulin in chicory roots may reduce appetite and assist in weight loss. Inulin also promotes beneficial gut bacteria. In addition, chicory is thought to boost immunity, lower LDL cholesterol, reduce anxiety, and provide various other health benefits. And you thought it could only be used to brew coffee!

Filling Your Basket

Chicory blooms between July and October, and the flowers are best harvested then. First, pick the flowers from the stems or cut them off with scissors. The leaves and stems are extraordinarily bitter, so harvest them when they are young. They are less bitter in spring and fall. Pick the seeds any time from late summer to early fall before they disperse or are lost to wind and weather.

The roots should be harvested in the fall. Use a garden spade or trowel and dig carefully around the base of the plant and the root to loosen it. Ensure that you do not bruise or nick the root. This could take a while, as some larger plants may have taproots up to two feet long (Dodrill, 2022).

Forest to Table

You can eat young leaves raw in salads but be warned: They are very bitter. Although cooking reduces the bitterness, a little goes a long way. Chicory greens are tasty when sautéed with onions and garlic.

The flowers are not as bitter as the leaves. Eat them raw and add them to salads, summer drinks, fruit salads, and desserts. Mix them into a jelly for a bitter-sweet taste sensation.

Use chicory roots to brew coffee. After cleaning the root thoroughly, roast pieces in the oven at 170° F for about 6–7 hours. Cut them as finely as possible to help them dry quickly. Use half a teaspoon of chicory root per cup (Dodrill, 2022).

Chicory intensifies the flavor of sugar and is used in baking to bump up the flavor.

PLEASE LEAVE A REVIEW

H i! What do you think of the information about the 11 edible wild plants that you've read so far? Is this book helping you?

If it is, would you help me find other people that this book can help? Please leave a review at https://bit.ly/review31ediblewildplantsbook

Or scan this QR code:

By taking two minutes to leave a review, you can make a difference for beginning foragers to find this resource that can help them on their path. Thank you in advance for your kindness!

FREE BONUS GIFT !

31 Edible Wild Plants: Forager's Field Notes and Photo Guide is ready for you to download and print!

It contains a photo and sketch for each of the 31 plants. Also, there are lined pages for your notes about characteristics of each plant, where you find it, and how you cook or prepare it.

Get **31 Edible Wild Plants: Forager's Field Notes and Photo Guide** by scanning the QR code below, or at this link:

https://foragersfieldnotes.ck.page/ca1889abf0

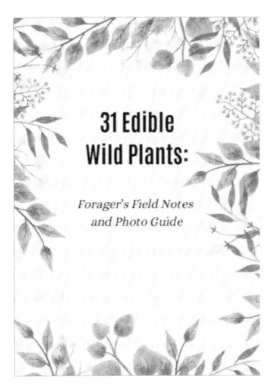

CLOVER

THE LUCK OF THE IRISH

What's in a Name?

Plant Family: Fabaceae

Botanical Names: *Trifolium repens; Trifolium pratense*

Common Names: White clover, Dutch clover, red clover, shamrock

In Irish, the word *seamog*, translated as "shamrock," means "summer plant." The name is thought to refer to the white or Dutch clover.

https://bit.ly/Clover_31EWP

Did You Know?

Initially considered sacred by the druids because of their trifoliate leaves, white or Dutch clover is the shamrock associated with Ireland and St. Patrick's Day. When Patrick came to Ireland, he used it to explain the Holy Trinity. An enduring myth is that finding a four-leaf clover will bring you good luck.

Red clover arrived in North America from Europe and Asia in the 18th century, where it was and still is used as a fodder crop (Ellis, 2019). It is a nitrogen-fixer that replenishes nitrogen in the soil, controls erosion, and provides nectar for honeybees. Because it is are rich in nutrients, widespread, and abundant, clover is an excellent famine crop. North American species include red, white, strawberry, alsike, and hop clover.

White and red clover are the species most commonly grown as cover crops and for livestock fodder. Milk is richer and creamier when clover is planted in dairy cow pastures. The more these plants are mowed, the more they grow. Clover grows in several soil types and climates and is ideal for composting. It prefers a combination of sun and shade. Considered a weed when it grows in lawns, clover is also commonly found along roadsides and the edges of farm fields.

Plant Description

Clover is an herbaceous perennial plant about 4–6 inches tall, with a spread of about 12 inches or more (N.C. Extension, n.d.). Its stems root freely, and it may form dense mats. It dies back slightly in winter but grows prolifically in the warmer months.

Leaves are trifoliate (three-lobed) and compound, with stipules attached to the leaf stalk. The leaves are arranged alternately on stems.

Flowers are five-petaled, with an ovary attached to the receptacle above the other flower parts (New World Encyclopedia, n.d.). The flower heads consist of crowded spikes of small, fragrant, colored flowers.

Seeds grow in pods derived from the calyx of the flower.

Look-Alike Plants

The common wood sorrel, *Oxalis acetosella*, is a garden weed that grows from a small rhizome. Some species have trifoliate leaves resembling clover, but their mauve flowers are very different.

Wholesome Goodness

Clover is high in protein. While the leaves and stalks are edible, they are hard to digest when raw. Juicing or boiling them for 5–10 minutes usually solves the problem (New World Encyclopedia, n.d.).

Clover has traditionally been used to treat skin conditions such as eczema and psoriasis. It is also considered an anticarcinogenic herb; doctors began prescribing it in the 1930s to treat certain cancers (Roberts, 2012). Clover tea can be taken for a variety of ailments.

Filling Your Basket

Leaves can be picked by hand or cut off the plant with scissors. Plants die back somewhat in the winter and yield fewer leaves than in the summer.

Clover flowers throughout the summer, with the first buds appearing in late spring. If warmer weather persists, the plants may bloom into the fall. Flower heads can be picked to eat fresh or dry for later use.

Seedpods are also edible and can be harvested by hand from the plants as they form.

Forest to Table

Clover leaves and flowers give salads a fresh, sweet taste. Add them to stir-fries and use them in sauces and garnishes.

Grind a mixture of dried seedpods and flowers to make nutritious flour.

CURLY DOCK

THE PERENNIAL THAT LOVES WATER

What's in a Name?

Family: Polygonaceae

Botanical Name: *Rumex crispus*

Common Name: Curly dock, yellow dock

The Latin word *crispus* means "curly," while dock refers to the practice of docking, or removing, an animal's tail.

Did You Know?

Curly dock originated in Europe around 500 BC (Lewis, 2004) and has long been used for food. The Greeks and Romans utilized curly dock for everything from dysentery to skin

https://bit.ly/ CurlyDock_31EWP

ailments to toothache. Dock leaves were fed to poultry and added to tobacco pouches to keep the tobacco moist. Plant stems were boiled and salted to weave into baskets. European women used curly dock seeds as fertility charms.

Since this plant belongs to the buckwheat family, its grain is very similar. Curly dock is a persistent perennial that can be harvested year-round. All aboveground parts are edible, although it is regarded as an invasive species in many parts of the world.

For a forager, one of the most wonderful things about curly dock is that it can grow practically everywhere, as long as the soil has some moisture. It is common in urban areas, gardens, roadsides, abandoned fields, and at the edges of forests.

Cautions

- Dock, like spinach, contains oxalic acid, which can be toxic in large quantities.
- Be assured, though, that there is no danger whatsoever if you limit the amount you eat to the same as a portion of spinach.

Plant Description

Curly dock is an upright, herbaceous perennial reaching 1–3 feet when mature (Lewis, 2004). It prefers sunny, moist locations and may be evergreen in certain climates. It has a single taproot with a dark yellow interior.

Leaves grow initially from the base of the plant, forming a rosette about one foot wide. In late spring, a flowering stalk sprouts from the rosette. The stalk is round, hairless, and ribbed, bearing leaves six inches long and one inch wide, arranged alternately (Illinois Wildflowers, n.d.). These leaves are hairless and dark green with lightly toothed, curly margins. The basal leaves look similar but are larger and less curly.

Flowers bloom in summer for about a month and form an inflorescence that is a panicle with whorls of flowers. Plants carry both male and female flowers because they are wind pollinated. The green or yellowish-green flowers consist of three inner and outer sepals, six stamens, three styles, and an ovary (Illinois Wildflowers, n.d.). There are no petals, and the flowers are unscented since they do not need to attract insects and bees.

Fruits are derived from the flowers, with each flower forming a single dry fruit containing one seed (Illinois Wildflowers, n.d.). The fruits and plant stems turn brown as they mature. Seeds are spread by wind or water.

Look-Alike Plants

Broadleaf dock and red sorrel, two other wild edibles, are the plants most likely to be confused with curly dock.

Wholesome Goodness

Curly dock has an excellent nutrition profile. In addition to vitamin B1, B2, and iron, it contains more vitamin C than oranges and more vitamin K than carrots.

Curly dock often grows near nettle, which is convenient since its leaves are said to relieve nettle stings. Dock roots are antibacterial, antifungal, antidiabetic (type 2), laxative, and diuretic. Dry and cure the roots for about 8–12 months to allow the medicinal compounds to mature (Vorderbruggen, 2006).

Filling Your Basket

If you want to enjoy the delicious flavor of dock leaves, harvest them early in the spring before they become bitter. They are curled tightly inward and should stretch when you pull on them, indicating that they are still tender and supple. Later in the season, when the leaves become dry and tear when you pull on them, they are unsuitable for consumption.

Harvest flower stalks in spring and early summer before they toughen. You can also eat the leaf stalks. Cut the shoots off at the base, or cut off the soft tops if it is later in the season. Strip off the leaves and peel off the tough outer layer.

Forest to Table

Use the young leaves raw in salads. Cook curly dock as you would spinach or kale. Steaming, boiling, or sautéing will improve the flavor of large leaves. You can also mix it with milder greens. Eat the leaf stalks raw; they taste similar to rhubarb.

After stripping the hard outer sheath from the stem, you should have a mildly-flavored light green shoot that can be eaten raw or cooked.

DANDELION

THE FLOWER WITH MEDITERRANEAN ROOTS

What's in a Name?

Family Name: Asteraceae

Botanical Name: *Taraxacum officinale*

Common Names: Dandelion, lion's tooth

Dandelion means "lion's tooth," referring to its jagged leaves.

Did You Know?

One sign of spring is when dandelions start blooming, often on your lawn. Unless you mow your lawn religiously, you probably won't have to go far to forage these "weeds." But despite the plant's bad reputation, dandelion leaves, flowers, and roots are all edible.

https://bit.ly/ Dandelion_31EWP

Dandelions are thought to have originated in the Mediterranean. The ancient Greeks, Romans, and Egyptians all used dandelions. In Chinese medicine, dandelions were used to detoxify the blood, act as a gentle diuretic, and improve the digestive system. In the 16th century, dandelion was recognized as an official medicine. Eighteenth-century Welsh doctors recommended them as a cure-all cleanser (Roberts, 2012).

One theory of how this prolific plant first arrived in North America is that immigrants brought them to plant in their herb gardens.

Dandelions provide nectar for bees and other pollinators, particularly in spring, before most other flowers start blooming. Birds feast on the fluffy seed heads. Finally, the sight of dainty dandelion seeds escaping into the wind delights children and the young at heart.

Cautions

- Dandelions are regarded as "slightly toxic," so do not use them continuously for long periods.
- Also, be careful to harvest dandelions from places that have not been treated with insecticides or herbicides.

Plant Description

Dandelions are hardy, perennial plants that withstand cold, frost, heat, drought, and crowding. In other words, dandelions can grow almost anywhere, whether or not you want them. They have milky sap and a single taproot, usually 6–12 inches long, which helps break up compacted soils and allows the dandelion to compete with other plants (Wisconsin Horticulture, 2022).

Their lance-shaped leaves emerge in spring and form a rosette at the base of the plant. Individual leaves may be toothed or lobed, with different lobe patterns occurring on the same plant. The leaves range from 5 to 25 inches long (Weed Science Society of America, n.d.).

Each yellow flower is 1 or 2 inches in diameter, perching cheerily atop a hollow flower stalk (Weed Science Society of America, n.d.). The single inflorescence consists of numerous ray and disc florets joined together in a way that resembles a daisy. The length of the flower stalk varies depending on environmental conditions.

Seed heads form the familiar globes. Each seed has a pappus, a feathery parachute of soft, white hairs that makes it easy for the wind to transport. Dandelion plants can produce up to 20,000 viable seeds each (Wisconsin Horticulture, 2022). Dandelions also reproduce vegetatively from pieces of taproot.

Look-Alike Plants

Several plants resemble the dandelion. These include chicory, cat's ear, sow thistle, and wild lettuce, all of which are edible.

Wholesome Goodness

Dandelion greens contain beta carotene, folate, thiamine, riboflavin, calcium, iron, potassium, manganese, and vitamins A, B6, C, E, and K.

Medicinally, dandelion is primarily a detoxifier and a diuretic. It soothes joint ailments, clears gout, and relieves fevers, insomnia, and constipation. Dandelion flowers and leaves harvested in early spring are considered a tonic. The milky sap in the flower stem can be used to remove warts.

Filling Your Basket

Dandelions usually peak in spring and fall, although they grow all year in warmer climates. Young leaves harvested in spring are less bitter. Look for leaves with fewer lobes because these have more flavor.

Flowers should be picked in the morning after the dew has dried. Use them as soon as possible or freeze them for later use.

Early fall is the best time to harvest the taproot. Simply pull it out of the ground with your hands or use a small garden fork or shovel. Wearing gardening gloves is recommended.

Forest to Table

Eat the leaves in salads, as a fresh vegetable, or steamed. Grind fresh leaves for dandelion pesto, adding lemon juice to relieve the bitterness. Dandelion also goes well with eggs.

Unlike the leaves, the flowers taste sweet. You can add them to sweet or savory baked goods or use them to make tea or jelly.

DAYLILY

THE BRIEF BUT BEAUTIFUL BLOOM

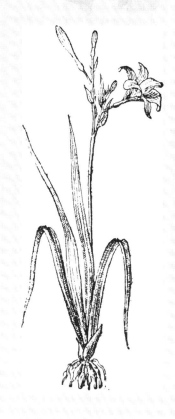

What's in a Name?

Plant Family: Asphodelaceae
Botanical Name: *Hemerocallis fulva*
Common Names: Daylily

The name is derived from the Greek words *hemera* and *kalis*, which mean "day" and "beautiful." This is probably a reference to the fact that the blooms only last a day. The species name, *fulva,* refers to the daylily's shades of orange, yellow, and auburn.

*https://bit.ly/
Daylily_31EWP*

Did You Know?

Daylilies were originally eaten in China, Japan, and surrounding countries. The earliest record of their cultivation there dates back to 2697 BC. They were brought to Europe from the Ottoman Empire around the 1500s and to North America after the Second Opium War. Some modern varieties date back 1,000 years (Keeler, 2018)! In China, pregnant women are encouraged to wear daylilies in their girdles to give birth to boys.

Popular with gardeners and landscapers, these beautiful flowers, once mainly orange or yellow, now display every color imaginable. When foraging for them in gardens, verify that the plants have not been sprayed with pesticides before you harvest them.

Daylilies, which thrive in full sun or partial shade, grow wild in forest thickets, grasslands, meadows, woodland borders, cemeteries, abandoned homesteads, and old flower gardens. They adorn the edges of footpaths, roads, railway lines, and stream banks.

DNA tests recently revealed that these plants are not actually lilies, despite the similarities in appearance.

Cautions

- Daylilies can be hallucinogenic in large quantities, so limit your intake.
- They are also toxic to cats.

Plant Description

The orange daylily is a deciduous, frost-hardy, perennial plant that forms clumps and grows 2–4 feet tall (Health Benefits Times, 2020). It has rhizomes and fleshy roots that are shaped like spindles and bear small tubers.

Leaves are shaped like swords, growing in pairs from the base of the plant. They are over a foot long, narrow, smooth, and slightly folded, with a central ridge running lengthwise down the back (Health Benefits Times, 2020).

Flowers form on the end of a long flower stem. Plants bear clusters of 10–20 short-stalked flowers. Only one opens at a time. The flowers are large, about three and a half inches across. Wild varieties are orange, yellow, or amber. Each flower has six tepals (3 petals and 3 sepals that look alike) united at the base but spreading out towards the tips. The flower's throat is yellow, surrounded by a red ring, while the rest is orange. Six long stamens and a single style extend from the center. Buds are green or greenish-orange, oblong, and about three inches long (Health Benefits Times, 2020).

Seeds occur in rows in a three-lobed, cylindrical seed capsule. They are infertile in orange daylilies, as the plants are sterile. Plants spread vegetatively through the roots, often displacing other species.

Look-Alike Plants

Plants with some similarities include Ontario blazing star, orange coneflower, and hairy beard's tongue.

Wholesome Goodness

Daylily flowers are rich in vitamin A and a good source of iron. In addition, they contain protein, fat, and carbohydrates.

Eating fresh flowers, leaves, and shoots may relieve anxiety and ease depression and sorrow.

In the late 19th century, daylilies were considered natural painkillers. Daylily tea was taken to alleviate rheumatism, aching joints, and cramps and used as a mouthwash to relieve toothache and oral infections.

Filling Your Basket

Daylilies bloom in July and August. Pick these flowers as soon as you see them since they only last one day.

Leaves should be harvested while young, before they become too fibrous.

Forest to Table

Young, tender daylily leaves and shoots can be eaten like asparagus or celery. They must be blanched and cooked before eating to reduce the compounds that cause hallucinations. Do not consume too many at once.

Flower buds have a flavor similar to peas. They are delicious in salads and stir-fries.

Eat the flowers raw or cooked. Raw, they are slightly crunchy, with a bit of sweetness at the base from the nectar. They taste similar to green beans. Steam or fry flowers and buds to complement any dish. If you wish to dehydrate the flowers, or use them as a thickener in food, pick them when they are closed and slightly withered.

You can also eat the small root tubers, which have a nutty flavor. Young tubers are best, although older tubers can be eaten as well.

EVENING PRIMROSE

THE BIENNIAL THAT OPENS AT NIGHT

What's in a Name?

Family: Onagraceae

Botanical Name: *Oenothera biennis*

Common Names: Evening primrose, sundrop, king's cure-all, evening star

This plant received its name because its flowers open in the evening and only last until the following noon.

Did You Know?

https://bit.ly/
EveningPrimrose_31EWP

Evening primrose is biennial. In its second year, it sends up a long flowerhead bearing masses of dainty, pale yellow flowers. It is native to North America and was unintentionally exported to Europe in the 1600s (Sweet, 2020). Indigenous Americans used evening primrose for food and medicine s far back as the 15th century (Roberts, 2012). All plant parts were eaten, and the roots, which were particularly valued, were stored in winter.

https://bit.ly/
EveningPrimroseRoots_31EWP

Evening primrose is a tough, drought-resistant plant that will grow anywhere sunny. Look for it in open fields, abandoned gardens, railway embankments, and waste ground.

The flowers can be clearly observed opening at night. The sphinx moth, which is nocturnal, is thought to pollinate the flowers. During the day, while flowers are still open, they are visited by hummingbirds and various butterflies and bees. Songbirds eat the seeds once the seedpods form.

Cautions

- Although evening primrose is not toxic, the uncooked leaves and roots could cause discomfort for some people who are sensitive to compounds in the plant

- People with epilepsy should not eat it or use it medicinally.

Plant Description

Leaves in the form of a rosette are produced from the base of the plant during its first year. Leaves are lance-shaped, about 3–7 inches long, and approximately 1–2 inches wide (Wikipedia, 2022). The leaf arrangement on the flower stalk is alternate, and the leaves are stalkless.

In the second year, the plants send out a flower shoot just over five feet tall (Wikipedia, 2022). Flowers are yellow, about 1–2 inches in diameter, with four lobed petals (Wikipedia, 2022). Each bloom has a bright nectar guide, visible only under ultraviolet light, and pollinators make a beeline for those. Flowers are grouped towards the top of the stem.

Fruit is a capsule, ¾–1.5 inches long, containing numerous tiny elongated seeds (Wikipedia, 2022). When mature, the capsule splits into four to release the seeds.

Look-Alike Plants

Goldenrod may be mistaken for evening primrose in the field. However, the evening primrose flower stem is much wider and the leaves longer than those of goldenrod. Also, goldenrod bears clusters of tiny, furry, gold-colored flowers in late summer.

Wholesome Goodness

Evening primrose leaves contain flavonoids, mucilage, tannins, and sugars. The seeds are tiny and take a lot of effort to harvest, but to compensate for the work they contain significant amounts of potassium, calcium, and healthy omega-3 fatty acids.

The most valued nutrient in evening primrose seeds is gamma linoleic acid (GLA), which is not found in any other food. GLA is a polyunsaturated fatty acid essential for forming compounds that ensure the proper functioning of human cells and is typically produced by the body.

Evening primrose is well known for relieving PMS. The oil is usually taken in capsule form. The flowers, leaves, and stem "bark" possess calming, almost sedative properties and help alleviate persistent coughs. In addition, medicinal tea can be made with the flowers.

Filling Your Basket

Eat the leaves during the first and second year of the plant's growth, before it flowers. Flowers bloom from June to September and can be eaten as well.

The taproot should be harvested in the fall or winter of the plant's first year. Once the flower stalk develops, the root becomes fibrous and inedible. The roots are long, reddish, and challenging to pull out without breaking.

Forest to Table

Eat the leaves raw or cooked. However, they are slightly hairy and not to everyone's liking. Try a small amount first.

Evening primrose flowers are a sweet-tasting delicacy. Use them as salad garnishes and in stir-fries and similar dishes. The buds can also be eaten raw.

The most popular edible part of the plant is undisputably the taproot. Peel it before cooking and add it to soups and stews like a potato.

FIELD PENNYCRESS

THE MUSTARD THAT ISN'T YELLOW

What's in a Name?

Plant Family: Brassicaceae
Botanical Name: *Thlaspi arvense*
Common Names: Field pennycress, French weed, bastard cress, mithridate mustard, fanweed, stinkweed

The common name refers to the seeds, which are shaped like old English pennies.

Did You Know?

Field pennycress is easy to identify in the field due to its large, abundant fruit and rank odor. Native to the Mediterranean region, field pennycress has spread worldwide. It arrived in North America in the early 1700s and was already classified as a weed by 1818. It spread to Canada in the 1860s, probably through contaminated animal fodder (Weed Science Society of America, 2022).

https://bit.ly/
Pennycress_31EWP

Since it grows year-round, pennycress can be considered a famine food. In addition, pennycress was considered a biofuel feedstock in the mid-2000s due to the high oil content of the seeds (Pennycress Resource Network, 2019). Researchers also investigated its potential as a soil biofumigant, and they are breeding useful cultivars.

This plant is a significant agricultural weed competing with crops. Spring floods spread the seeds over vast areas, contaminating soils. You will find it in grain, clover, and hay fields, grasslands, roadsides, and wastelands. A pioneer plant on bare ground, it readily invades cultivated lands. The plant grows as a rosette in the early stages, and the leaves protect it during winter. It loves the spring and summer sun.

Cautions

- The seeds contain a glycoside poisonous to animals and may taint cow's milk and livestock meat.
- Consume the seeds with caution, as large doses may reduce white blood cells and cause nausea and dizziness.
- Pregnant or breastfeeding women should not eat or use pennycress.
- Applying it directly to the skin may cause irritation.

Plant Description

Pennycress is an annual that prefers fertile sites but will grow in other places as well. The tall flower stem is unbranched or sparsely branched, growing to a height of 1.6–2.6 feet (Health Benefits Times, 2018).

Leaves grow in a rosette from the base in spring. They are spatula-shaped and wilt away early. Stem leaves are alternate, 1–4 inches long and up to one inch wide, hairless, with irregular blunt teeth and a rounded point at the tip (Health Benefits Times, 2018). The edges are often wavy. Leaves near the base of the plant may have short stems, while those near the top do not. When crushed, they have a mustardy aroma, which is very helpful for identification purposes.

Flowers occur near the top of the plant. They have four small, white, clawed petals that grow in dense clusters, lengthening with age. They have six stamens, divided into two sets on either side of the ovary. They have four sepals (Stephenson, 2021).

Fruits are round, flat, winged pods with a deep notch, measuring 0.39 inches across, borne on slender upward curving stalks (Health Benefits Times, 2018). They are initially bright green, turning yellowish and then brown as they mature.

Look-Alike Plants

Shepherd's purse, a related wild edible, may be confused with field pennycress. However, shepherd's purse is typically smaller and less dense, with triangular seedpods and no odor.

Wholesome Goodness

Field pennycress contains sulfur and vitamins C and G. The leaves are rich in protein.

It has a wide range of medicinal uses. The entire plant is antibacterial, anti-inflammatory, expectorant, and a blood tonic.

Filling Your Basket

Harvest the young leaves before the plant flowers, or they can be extremely bitter. You can also eat the flowers from May to July when plants bloom. Pennycress seeds develop in late spring and early summer. Seedpods readily shatter when they are ripe; harvest them by hand.

Forest to Table

Eat the young leaves and shoots cooked, or raw in salads. They tend to be bitter and are not to everyone's taste, however. Mix other leaves with them to counter the bitterness and use them in small quantities. Add them to lasagna and soups. Grind the seeds into a powder and use them as a mustard substitute. Sprout the seeds and add them to salads.

HOG PEANUT

THE VINY LEGUME

What's in a Name?

Plant Family: Fabaceae

Botanical Name: *Amphicarpaea bracteata*

Common Name: Hog peanut, American hog peanut

The common name refers to the fleshy fruits of the semi-fertile, edible flowers.

Did You Know?

Hog peanuts are native to North America and occur across the eastern U.S. Interestingly, they have two kinds of flowers and seeds. Hog peanuts are legumes and, therefore, nitrogen fixers. Their unusual fruits distinguish them from other vines in this plant family. Butterflies, caterpillars, beetles, birds, mice, and white-tailed deer feed on the foliage.

https://bit.ly/ HogPeanuts_31EWP

HOG PEANUT

Hog peanuts are generally found in moist places such as floodplain woodlands, wooded areas along streams, wet thickets, damp sandy meadows, and seeps. They also grow in disturbed ground, gardens, and cultivated soils. They prefer full sun to partially shady conditions.

Plant Description

This plant is a summer annual about 2.8 feet long (Illinois Wildflowers, n.d.). It is a vine without tendrils that twines itself around adjacent vegetation, branching occasionally. The slender, hairy stems are light green to reddish green.

Leaves are compound, occurring in groups of three at the end of a long stem. Leaflets are hairy with sharply pointed tips. The base is usually asymmetrical and may be rounded, tapering, and diamond or egg-shaped. The middle leaflet, which bears the leaf stalk, is larger than the other two, up to three inches long and two and a half inches wide (Minnesota Wildflowers, n.d.). The other two leaflets are stalkless.

The first type of hog peanut flower grows in a compact cluster of 2–15 flowers at the end of a long stem arising from a leaf axil (Minnesota Wildflowers, n.d.). Flowers are two inches long and have five petals, a tubular calyx with four teeth, several stamens, and a pistil. They resemble pea flowers. Plants are adorned with these pale pink, mauve, or white blooms from midsummer to fall for 1.5–3 months (Illinois Wildflowers, n.d.).

The second type of hog peanut flowers is self-fertile and inconspicuous, growing on ground-hugging stolons.

The fruit is a green peapod 1.5 inches long, containing 3–4 seeds (Minnesota Wildflowers, n.d.). Stolon flowers produce single-seeded, curved, fleshy fruits, which may become subterranean.

Look-Alike Plants

Groundnuts are from the same family but produce edible underground tubers that are part of the root system rather than modified seeds. This plant has compound leaves with five leaflets and flowers that are usually reddish-brown. Other vines in the bean family have different-shaped flowers and broader leaflets.

Wholesome Goodness

The subterranean hog peanut fruits are a good protein and carbohydrate source.

Swelling may be relieved by a poultice made with hog peanut leaves, while an infusion of the root may help settle an upset stomach. Externally, the root has been applied to rattlesnake bites.

Filling Your Basket

The subterranean pods are difficult to find but well worth the effort. Harvest them throughout the winter. Gather the aboveground pods from late summer through fall. While the roots are considered edible, opinions differ on whether they are palatable. Pull some up in fall and winter if you decide to taste them for yourself.

Forest to Table

Eat the underground seeds raw or cooked as a peanut substitute. They taste somewhat like green beans. Yields are relatively low, but they make a delicious and nutritious snack. The aboveground seedpods are much smaller. Cook them before eating and use them like lentils. If you find roots large enough to be worth harvesting, peel and boil them before eating.

HONEYSUCKLE

THE SWEET AND SCENTED

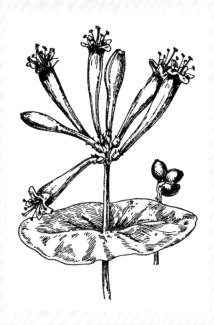

What's in a Name?

Plant Family: Caprifoliaceae

Botanical Name: *Lonicera sempervirens*

Common Names: Coral honeysuckle, trumpet honeysuckle, woodbine

The genus name *lonicera* refers to the 16th-century botanist Adam Lonitzer. The name of the species comes from two Latin words, *semper* and *virens*, meaning "always green." Honeysuckle refers to the sweet nectar that can be sucked from the flowers.

Did You Know?

https://bit.ly/
Honeysuckle_31EWP

These gorgeous plants need no introduction. Even if you're not a forager, you've probably picked the small, trumpet-like flowers to suck nectar from the base. When in full bloom, honeysuckle shrubs fill the air with their scent, especially in the evenings.

There are approximately 180 species of honeysuckle worldwide, with over half growing in China (Fruits Info, 2022). The stems often fold in on themselves and can be used to make walking sticks. During the Bronze Age, people used honeysuckle vines as rope. It was once believed that if the plant grew at the entrance to a home, it would bring good luck and prevent evil spirits from entering.

Honeysuckle is native to the eastern U.S. but occurs as far west as Texas. It is most common in the Southeast. It is on the threatened species list in Maine and considered rare in Rhode Island. While plants are resistant to drought and cold, they prefer moist and sunny locations and are most common in coastal regions. The flowers, with their sweet nectar, attract bees, butterflies, and hummingbirds. Several bird species eat the berries. Small mammals may use the plants for cover. Find these plants in forests and gardens or along fences, hedges, and roads. Do not cultivate honeysuckle near buildings since it is extremely flammable.

Cautions

Some honeysuckle species are inedible and may even be poisonous. Therefore, make 100% sure of your identification before foraging this plant.

Plant Description

Coral honeysuckle is a woody perennial shrub with taproots. It grows like a vine, twining around fences and other plants, and may reach 20 feet long (Wikipedia, 2021). When cultivated, it may grow like a ground cover. It is characterized by its scarlet, trumpet-shaped flowers.

Leaves are semi-evergreen and simple. They grow in opposite pairs and are oval, up to two inches long and one and a half inches wide (Wikipedia, 2021). The leaves immediately below the flowers have leaf stalks joined at the base to form a ring around the shoot.

Flowers grow in whorled clusters of 2–4 tubular blossoms at the ends of new growth stems. They are about two inches long, red outside and yellow inside (TWC Staff, 2019). Five small lobes open at the tip, exposing the stamens and stigma. Clusters are usually grouped together in threes (Wikipedia, 2021).

Fruits are tiny red berries less than half an inch in circumference (Wikipedia, 2021). They are inedible and are produced from late summer into the fall.

Look-Alike Plants

Honeysuckle cannot really be confused with other plants. However, some varieties are invasive species in the U.S. Two examples are amur honeysuckle and Japanese honeysuckle, which bears predominantly yellow or white flowers and dark blue-black berries and is used in landscaping or gardens.

Another edible variety is pink honeysuckle (*lonicera hispidula*), native to the western U.S. and Canada.

Wholesome Goodness

The flowers contain mostly water but are a good source of dietary fiber and vitamin C. They also contain vitamin B1 and some potassium. Other nutrients available in trace amounts include vitamins B2 and B6, calcium, copper, iron, magnesium, manganese, phosphorus, potassium, sodium, and zinc.

Make honeysuckle tea from fresh or dried flowers to relieve headaches, fevers, sunstroke, hot flashes, sore throats, colds, flu, and digestive problems.

Filling Your Basket

Honeysuckle usually blooms throughout the summer, beginning as early as March in some locations. When harvesting, leave some flowers for the hummingbirds, bees, and butterflies. Pick open blooms, cutting them off the vine without cutting the base of the flowers so that you preserve the sweet nectar within.

Forest to Table

Before using the flowers, remove any stems and the calyx (the green part at the base) to avoid bitterness and improve flavor. Then, leave them on a tray outside for half an hour to allow insects to depart.

Garnish salads, fruit salads, and desserts with honeysuckle flowers. Make them into sweet syrup or jelly and add them to cakes. Combining the flowers with fresh mint, olive oil, and vinegar makes a delicious salad dressing. Flowers can also be dried for later use.

JAPANESE KNOTWEED

THE NUTRITIOUS OUTLAW

What's in a Name?

Plant Family: Polygonaceae
Botanical Name: *Fallopia japonica*
Common Names: Japanese knotweed, Japanese bamboo, Mexican bamboo, Japanese fierce flower, crimson beauty, Hancock's curse

Did You Know?

Japanese knotweed is native to Southeast Asia. It was introduced to North America in the late 1800s as a garden plant to control erosion. However, it escaped cultivation and by the early 1900s had become an invasive, noxious weed (Minnesota Department of Agriculture, n.d.). It even grows through concrete and tar, damaging infrastructure.

https://bit.ly/ JapaneseKnotweed_31EWP

Cultivation, propagation, and transportation of Japanese knotweed are outlawed in several U.S. states.

Despite the bad press, Japanese knotweed is edible and nutritious, containing powerful antioxidants. Its blossoms attract beneficial insects such as bees, butterflies, and wasps. Some beekeepers consider it a valuable nectar source for bees when little else flowers. In addition, resveratrol extracted from Japanese knotweed is used to produce an organic fungicide spray for crops.

https://bit.ly/ JapaneseKnotweed2_31EWP

Japanese knotweed occurs in sunny spots in gardens, parks, landscaped areas, roadsides, and damp places such as riverbanks, wetlands, wet depressions, and woodland margins. It reproduces by seed. In North America, Japanese knotweed only bears female flowers. However, it will produce viable seeds if giant or Bohemian

knotweed is nearby to provide a pollen source. The plants also reproduce vegetatively through their rhizomes.

Cautions

- As there are concerted efforts to eradicate it, take care where
  you harvest Japanese knotweed. Ensure that it has not been
  treated with chemical herbicides.
- Even fragments can grow into new plants, so be careful
  when discarding rhizome pieces.
- The plants contain oxalic acid. Do not eat them if you
  cannot eat rhubarb.

Plant Description

These plants are perennial herbaceous shrubs that grow to about 9
feet (Minnesota Department of Agriculture, n.d.). Although the
stems may die in winter, the woody stalks persist. The stems are
hollow, rounded, and upright, with a papery membrane. Japanese
knotweed forms tall, dense, bamboo-like thickets that shade out and
displace native vegetation, degrade habitat for fish and wildlife, alter
waterways, and encourage flooding. It contains compounds that
suppress the growth of nearby plants and interfere with nitrogen
availability in wetlands.

Leaves are simple, alternate, and broad, up to five inches long and
four inches wide, with sharply-pointed tips and flat bases (MISIN,
2020).

Flowers are small, greenish-white, and very numerous. They are
borne on a slender stalk near the end of the stems.

Fruits are small, three-winged, dark, and glossy (Minnesota Department of Agriculture, n.d.). The seeds float easily and are dispersed by
wind and water.

Look-Alike Plants

Dogwood and lilac are often confused with Japanese knotweed, but they are woody plants, not herbaceous. Also, dogwood and lilac leaves are arranged oppositely on their stems, while the leaf arrangement on Japanese knotweed is alternate.

Houttuynia is another look-alike, but it's only about one foot high (Phlorum, 2021).

Ornamental bistort is planted purposefully and doesn't spread wildly. Its leaves are larger than knotweed leaves, stems are much thicker and shorter, and flowers form clusters.

Lesser knotweed has long, thin leaves and is much shorter. Flowers are bigger and clearly bell-shaped.

Himalayan balsam has longer, thinner leaves with a pale pink midrib. It flowers in mid to late summer, and flowers are large, pink, hooded, and lipped. Their seedpods explode when touched.

Bamboo has long, slender leaves and stiff stems that cannot be snapped like those of Japanese knotweed.

Wholesome Goodness

Japanese knotweed is rich in vitamins A and C and contains manganese, phosphorus, zinc, and potassium.

Its rhizomes contain resveratrol, a phenolic compound of medical interest due to its antioxidant activity. Therefore, knotweed may improve immunity and even help combat the bacteria that cause Lyme disease.

Filling Your Basket

The best time to cut shoots is early spring, when they are tender and edible. If you harvest them later, they will be tougher and need to be peeled before eating. You can also eat the leaves. However, they become very bitter as spring advances. The rhizomes can be used medicinally.

Forest to Table

Leaves and young shoots taste like a cross between asparagus and rhubarb. Boil or steam them like young asparagus or eat them chilled, with dressing. They can be used as a rhubarb substitute in dessert recipes. Use them in pies, soups, sauces, jams, chutneys, and wine.

Peel mature shoots before eating. Prepare them any way you like, including grilling, sautéing, and pickling.

LAMBSQUARTERS

THE SHEEP WITH A GOOSEFOOT

What's in a Name?

Plant Family: Chenopodiaceae

Botanical Name: *Chenopodium album*

Common Names: Wild spinach, lambsquarters, goosefoot, fat hen, melde

The common name refers to Lammas Quarter, an ancient English festival held when the plant was harvested. In the 19th century, tenants of the Archbishop of York had to bring a lamb to the altar, which could also explain the name (Banker, 2020). The word *cheno* means "goose"," *podium* means "foot," and *album* means "white." The botanical name, therefore, refers to the shape of the leaf, which resembles a goose's foot. The underside of the leaf is white, hence "white goosefoot."

https://bit.ly/ Lambsquarters_31EWP

Did You Know?

Before spinach, there was lambsquarters. Neolithic, Bronze Age, and early Iron Age people ate it as a vegetable until spinach was imported from Southeast Asia in the 16th century (Weed Science Society of America, n.d.). In an odd quirk, one of its common names today is "wild spinach!" Lambsquarters was eaten by the Anglo-Saxons, who called it "melde" and named towns after it because it grew so abundantly. Lambsquarters arrived in North America via Asia and Europe. The Blackfoot tribe ate the plant and used it for medicine.

In the U.S. today, it's regarded as a weed, although it covers abandoned lands and can be considered a soil protector. Lambsquarters is related to quinoa and cultivated for food in India. The seeds can be used for grain.

Lambsquarters grows along fences, sidewalks, and roadsides. It is typically found in disturbed places, including landscaped yards, agricultural lands, stream banks, gardens, and wastelands. The presence of lambsquarters indicates good soil. It grows in full to partial sun and can tolerate cold and mild frost.

Plant Description

From a distance, plants look dusty, as the underside of the leaves is covered with a white, powdery, and waxy coating. This helps the plant to stay hydrated and is a distinguishing characteristic of lambsquarters.

Lambsquarters is an herbaceous summer annual. Older plants look lush and dense due to their many branches. They are generally 3–5 feet tall but occasionally grow as high as seven feet (Sycamore, 2018). Mature stems are vertically grooved with red, pink, purple, yellow, or green stripes. The plant has a short, branched taproot.

Leaves vary in shape from triangular and goosefoot-shaped to oval. They are soft, velvety, and about 3–6 inches long and 1–2 inches wide

(Tesolin, 2021). Young plants have opposite leaves that become alternate as the stem grows. The leaves radiate out from the stem in a starburst shape.

Flowers are tiny, greenish, and densely grouped in small, thick, granular clusters along the main stem and upper branches. They have five green sepals but no petals (Stephenson, 2021).

Seeds are very small, rounded, and flattened. Lambsquarters seeds prolifically, with one plant producing 72,000 seeds (Tesolin, 2021).

Look-Alike Plants

Lambsquarters is closely related to orache, which is also edible.

Black nightshade is often mistaken for lambsquarters, as they sometimes grow near each other. However, the black nightshade plant has smoother egg-shaped leaves, and its flowers have petals. Its berries are slightly toxic.

Deadly nightshade is a dangerous, poisonous look-alike to black nightshade and lambsquarters. Its berries grow individually rather than in clusters, and the leaves are rounder. It also has petalled flowers.

Due to the risk, please be extra cautious and only harvest lambsquarters if you are sure you have identified it correctly.

Wholesome Goodness

Lambsquarters contains lots of essential vitamins and several amino acids. It is a good source of phosphorus, protein, trace minerals, vitamins A, C, and K, iron, calcium, copper, manganese, and potassium.

The plant has countless medicinal uses, including treating painful limbs, relieving digestive problems, and soothing burns.

Filling Your Basket

The leaves, shoots, flowers, and seeds are all edible. The seeds should not be eaten in excess, however, since they contain saponins and oxalic acid.

Harvest lambsquarters in spring when the shoots are young and tender before plants begin flowering. Snip off stems and leaves with scissors. When the stems become tough, harvest the tips.

Collect the seeds in the fall when seed heads are dry and brown. Rub them between your hands to remove the chaff and keep the seeds.

Forest to Table

Use lambsquarters in moderation, as the plant contains oxalic acid. Steam or boil lambsquarters like spinach or other leafy greens. Use it raw in salads, stir-fries, omelets, smoothies, soups, stews, and curries. It can also be fried or used as a pizza topping.

The seeds taste like buckwheat but are very hard. Grind them up to add to bread and other baked goods or make them into flour. The flour is dark but bakes well and is very nutritious.

MARSH MARIGOLD

THE SHINY GOLDEN GOBLET

What's in a Name?

Family Name: Ranunculaceae
Botanical Name: *Caltha palustris*
Common Names: Marsh marigold, cowslip, cowcup, kingcup

The genus name *caltha* derives from an old Greek word *kalathos*, meaning "goblet" or "cup." This describes the shape of the flowers with their upturned petals. *Palustris* means "of marshy areas," referring to the plant's habitat.

https://bit.ly/ MarshMarigold_31EWP

Did You Know?

You know spring is near when the marsh marigolds flower. From the buttercup family of plants, they develop beautiful deep yellow flowers in spring and early summer. Found throughout Canada and the northern U.S., marsh marigolds are a threatened species in the southern part of their range. They also occur in England, South America, and Australia. In addition to eating marsh marigolds as food, Indigenous American tribes used them to induce vomiting and counter love charms.

Queen Victoria was said to have enjoyed capers made from marsh marigold flower buds.

In the wild, marsh marigolds form gorgeous stands of bright green and deep yellow across the landscape. As the name suggests, these plants grow best in wet places—marshes, fens, ditches, damp woods, and swamps. They prefer full sun and light shade and are popular garden plants.

Cautions

- Always cook marsh marigold leaves, buds, flowers, and roots before eating because the whole plant contains the toxic glycoside protoanemonin. It is destroyed by heat, though, so the plant is safe to eat as long as it is cooked.
- Some individuals find that handling the plants causes skin irritation. Wear gloves when harvesting as a precaution.
- Cattle and horses may be poisoned by eating marsh marigolds, although dried plant material does not affect them.

Plant Description

Marsh marigolds are between 8 and 24 inches tall (Wild Plant Guides, 2021). They are herbaceous perennial herbs with hollow stems that grow over a foot long when bearing flowers (Trull, n.d.). The roots consist of short rhizomes.

The leaves are distinctive enough to identify this plant. The basal leaves are large, glossy, bright green, hairless, and kidney-shaped with crenate margins. They have a deep, narrow notch; whitish, netted veins; and are paler underneath. Basal leaves have long leaf stalks, while stem leaves have shorter ones and are alternately arranged. Stipules surround the stem like a sheath.

Flowers are showy, shiny, and bright yellow, occurring in clusters measuring half to one and a half inches across. They have 5–9 petal-like sepals. While these appear a uniform yellow to us, insects see an ultraviolet color in the upper parts of the sepals. Flowers have 50 to over 100 stamens and offer pollen and nectar to insect visitors (Trull, n.d.).

Fruits look like spiky crowns with 12 segments, each containing several tiny seeds (Wild Plant Guides, 2021).

Look-Alike Plants

Lesser celandine has leaves that emerge as early as February. While marsh marigolds are at the water's edge, lesser celandine is more adaptable. It may be found in drier areas further away. It also flowers earlier, bearing 7–11 petals and 3 green sepals below the blooms (Smirch, n.d.). Lastly, lesser celandine is invasive, forming enormous mats if unchecked. It has bulblets in the leaf axils that form new plants vegetatively.

Wholesome Goodness

Although marsh marigolds were once used in several traditional medicine preparations, there are no known medicinal uses for these plants today.

Filling Your Basket

Wear gloves when harvesting this plant, as the toxic glycoside can irritate the skin of sensitive individuals.

Harvest the new leaves by picking them off the plants. Marsh marigolds flower any time from mid-April to June, depending on how far north you are. Pick the flower buds.

Forest to Table

Boil the leaves and add them to salads and savory dishes such as lasagna, soup, and stew. Flower buds can be pickled like capers.

The roots can also be eaten after cooking or added to soups, stews, and similar dishes.

NANNYBERRY

THE FRUIT TO FIND IN WINTER

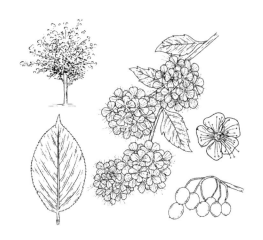

What's in a Name?

Family Name: Adoxaceae
Botanical Name: *Viburnum lentago*
Common Names: Nannyberry, sweet viburnum, blackhaw, wild raisin, sheepberry, nanny plum, sweetberry, tea plant

Lentago, Latin for "flexible," refers to the plant's tough, flexible twigs. The common name refers to nanny goats that feed on its berries. Some people call them "sheepberries" because overripe nannyberries smell like wet sheep wool.

https://bit.ly/ Nannyberry_31EWP

Did You Know?

Nannyberries should definitely be on your menu if you like foraging for sweet fruit. They're extremely sweet and available during fall and even winter, so you can harvest them throughout the cold season, especially further north. Also called sweet viburnum, these shrubs are native to the Midwestern and eastern U.S. and southern Canada. Indigenous Americans used nannyberries as an ingredient in herbal medicines.

Nannyberries yield plenty of fruit. They prefer moist soils and grow in shade to full sun. You will find them in rocky and mesic woodlands, low woodlands along streams, thickets, roadsides, fence rows, rocky hillsides, the edges of swamps, upland woods and hardwood forest margins, floodplains, and lakeshores. They are often used in urban landscaping and for hedges, while large shrubs and trees may form windbreaks on farms or in gardens. Birds and animals eat the ripe fruit, usually after the first frost. The wood is heavy, hard, close-grained, and somewhat smelly.

Plant Description

Nannyberries are deciduous perennial shrubs or small trees. They have both scattered, anchoring roots and shallow, fibrous roots that bind the soil. The roots have buds, which form aboveground stems or suckers. In ideal conditions, nannyberries form large dense colonies. Plants are leggy and open when mature, with an irregularly rounded crown, and have suckers at the base. The plant has many slender, flexible, round twigs, which are green on young plants and later turn brown. They may be covered with a whitish, waxy bloom and smell unpleasant when bruised.

Leaves are simple, opposite, and attached to the plant with a winged leaf stalk. They are relatively thin, broadly egg-shaped or elliptical, and about 2–4 inches long (Health Benefits Times, 2021). They have short, sharp teeth and wavy margins. They are glossy, dark green on top with a lighter underside, and become reddish-purple in fall.

Flowers are small, creamy-white, and occur in clusters at the tips of twigs at least a year old. These clusters have flat tops or slight domes and grow up to four and a half inches long. Individual flowers are small, about a quarter inch across, and bell or saucer shaped with five rounded lobes. In the center are a short style and five long yellow stamens that extend beyond the flower tube. The green calyx around the flower base has a short tube and five triangular lobes (Stephenson, 2021). Flower stalks are green to red and hairless.

Nannyberry fruits are actually drupes, lime green at first and then bright pink, turning dark bluish-black when ripe. They are about half an inch in diameter, oval to almost spherical (Health Benefits Times, 2021). A single large stone seed is found inside the drupe.

Look-Alike Plants

The highbush cranberry looks very similar, but its leaves have three lobes and its berries are dark red when ripe.

Northern wild raisins have much smaller fruit and are borne upright rather than dangling downwards like nannyberries. The raisins taste like, well, raisins. Wild raisins also ripen earlier and birds usually find them before foragers do.

The hobblebush has huge leaves, similar to those of basswood trees, and clusters of dark, black fruits which face upright.

All of the above are edible and have unique flavors.

Wholesome Goodness

Nannyberries are rich in antioxidants and contain protein, carbohydrates, fiber, calcium, potassium, and vitamins A, C, and D.

Medicinally, leaf infusions and root decoctions have been used to treat various ailments and health conditions. The bark is antispasmodic and is used in tea. The juice relieves digestive problems. An extract of the leaves, bark, and berries assists with respiratory and digestive ailments or menstrual problems.

Filling Your Basket

Nannyberry fruits ripen in stages, starting in early fall and ripening fully in early November. The season's first berries don't have much flavor, so you may want to wait to harvest sweeter and more flavorful fruits. Nannyberries tolerate cold and will remain on the plant through winter. Since most migratory birds leave by then, you'll have less competition for the fruit.

Forest to Table

The berries are easy to spot against the snow. Simply pick them off the branches and eat them. Be careful not to crack a tooth or swallow the hard seeds.

To process the nannyberries you bring home, remove the stems, leaves, and other debris from ripe berries. Boil them for about 20 minutes to separate the fruit from the seeds. Next, press the boiled berries through a food strainer to remove the seeds. This can only be done while the berries are hot, so work quickly. Finally, dry the puree by spreading it on a tray and baking in the oven at 300° F for 30–40 minutes (Adamant, 2019). Sweeten if desired, then bottle it and use it like jam.

Use nannyberries in teas or add them to pies, cakes, sorbets, and desserts. You can also dehydrate them.

OSTRICH FERN

THE FOREST FIDDLEHEAD

What's in a Name?

Plant Family: Onocleaceae

Botanical Name: *Matteuccia struthiopteris*

Common Name: Ostrich fern, shuttlecock fern, fiddlehead fern

The name of this species is derived from the ancient Greek words for "ostrich" and "fern." The ostrich fern is the only species in the *Matteuccia* genus.

Did You Know?

The young, curled leaves of ferns are called fiddleheads because they resemble the scroll on the neck of a violin or fiddle. These edible new shoots of ostrich ferns are a prized delicacy, costly and difficult to find even in specialty stores and upmarket restaurants. Yet foragers delight in their privilege of venturing into the wild to harvest them.

https://bit.ly/ OstrichFern_31EWP

Ostrich ferns are native to North America and are found in the northern U.S. and much of Canada. These ferns grow so rapidly that the fiddleheads are available for only about two weeks in spring (Moulton, 2022). So you only have a short foraging window to find and enjoy this gourmet food.

Most ferns grow fiddleheads, so identifying the correct one is important. In the wild, ostrich ferns prefer cool, damp weather and are partial to swamplands. They grow near rivers and streams in wet, rich soil. During their furled stage, they look like shoots poking out of the ground.

Cautions

Ostrich fern fiddleheads should never be eaten raw. They must be thoroughly boiled for at least 10 minutes before eating to break down a toxin that causes food poisoning (Gardening Channel, 2011).

Plant Description

Ostrich ferns are perennial plants that emerge from a clump known as a crown. The ferns usually cluster in groups of 3–12 near rivers and streams in April and May (Gardening Channel, 2011).

Fiddleheads emerge from a rhizome that breaks through the soil surface in spring. They are often surrounded by the brown papery remains of the previous year's growth, which are usually in the center.

Ostrich fern fiddleheads are about an inch in diameter. They have a brown, papery, scale-like covering on the uncoiled fern (Fuller, n.d.).

These flake off with the brush of a finger. If there are no brown papery coverings, or if the fiddleheads have wooly coverings, they are not ostrich ferns.

Another distinctive characteristic to help you identify an ostrich fern is the deep u-shaped groove on the inside of its otherwise smooth stem. It resembles a celery stalk, only much smaller.

Look-Alike Plants

The bracken fern does not have a noticeable stem groove or brown scales. Instead, they appear a bit fuzzy. Their most prominent characteristic is multiple stems on a single stalk. These fronds uncurl into the larger leaves typical of bracken ferns.

Lady ferns are very similar to ostrich ferns but have much darker, stickier scales, resembling old feathers rather than paper.

Cinnamon ferns have a wooly covering and flattened stalk instead of a grooved one.

Royal ferns have bright pink stems, with fiddleheads covered in brownish hairs.

Fiddleheads from all the ferns mentioned above are edible. However, cinnamon ferns should be cooked thoroughly before eating to avoid feeling nauseous or dizzy after consumption.

Wholesome Goodness

Fiddleheads contain carbohydrates, protein, and a little fat. They are an excellent source of vitamin K, folate, potassium, antioxidants, iron, and omega-3 fatty acids.

The fiddleheads of ostrich ferns are used medicinally to relieve sore throats, as a laxative, and for boils and wounds. There is no scientific evidence to support this, however.

Filling Your Basket

Pick ostrich fern fiddleheads in spring as they emerge from the crown. They are best harvested when they are 2–6 inches tall so a little of the tasty stem can be included. The fiddlehead will still be tightly curled. For sustainable harvesting, only take fiddleheads from healthy crowns with four fiddleheads rather than two. If there are only one or two fiddleheads, they may not be growing optimally or not yet established (Fuller, n.d.). Snap the fiddleheads off by hand or cut them off with a knife or sharp scissors. Take care not to damage the remaining fiddleheads.

To ensure sustainability, harvest only half the available fiddleheads. The rest should be allowed to grow to maturity, so you'll have a harvest next year.

Forest to Table

As mentioned previously, ostrich fern fiddleheads must be thoroughly boiled before eating. They taste like a combination of asparagus, green beans, and broccoli, with the texture of green beans, and are best eaten immediately after cooking. Steam or sauté them or add them to omelets and pasta dishes. Ostrich fern fiddleheads are the only ones that can be pickled.

They dry out when refrigerated but will keep for about two weeks. Frozen, they will last about six months (Berardi, n.d.).

PARSNIP

THE CARROT'S COUSIN

What's in a Name?

Plant Family: Apiaceae

Botanical Name: *Pastinaca sativa*

Common Name: Wild parsnip

Wild and cultivated parsnips are identical and have the same botanical name.

Did You Know?

Parsnips were eaten in ancient times in Europe and are believed to have originated in the Mediterranean. The Romans used parsnips for food and animal fodder and also to sweeten cakes and baked goods. The

https://bit.ly/ Parsnip_31EWP

Roman Emperor Tiberius was so fond of parsnips that he imported them from Germany, where they grew along the Rhine River. British colonists and settlers introduced parsnips to the New World, where

Indigenous Americans started growing them. However, with the introduction of potatoes and sugar, these plants declined in popularity.

Nevertheless, wild parsnips are still common in North America, especially in disturbed ground. They occur on roadsides, fields, pastures, and even your lawn. However, they proliferate in such a wide variety of environmental conditions that they are considered invasive. Despite this, they have high nutritional value and are worth harvesting. This is also probably one of the best ways to stop its spread.

Cautions

- Be careful when harvesting wild parsnips. All the aboveground parts and the sap contain a chemical that may cause severe burns on bare skin. This happens when the sap is exposed to sunlight. Even brushing against plants can release the toxin.
- Ensure that you cover all areas that could be exposed when harvesting. Wear long-sleeved shirts, long pants, boots, and long gloves.
- If you are allergic to mugwort, you might also react negatively to parsnips. Cooking them usually resolves this problem.
- It is also toxic to livestock if consumed.

Plant Description

Wild parsnips are herbaceous biennials/perennials. They are very invasive and toxic to humans and livestock. Mature plants are yellowish-green, with hollow, grooved stems similar to celery. In the first year they produce leafy rosettes. In the second year, they elongate to produce flowers and seeds. The flower stalk may reach five feet tall (Cornell Weed Identification, n.d.).

The rosette has low-growing clusters of compound leaves from 5–15 inches long. Leaves on the main stem, also compound, are between 6–12 inches long and consist of 3–5 toothed, diamond-shaped leaflets (Cornell Weed Identification, n.d.). Lower leaves have short stalks, while those further up are stalkless.

Parsnip flowers consist of a flat-topped umbel (umbrella-shaped flowerhead) with clustered yellow flowers on the ends. There is a single flower stalk branching off the stem. Each tiny flower has five petals (Cornell Weed Identification, n.d.). Flowers on the main stem bloom first, followed by those on the branches. This means the plant produces seeds for a longer time.

Seeds are initially bright green, maturing over about three weeks and gradually turning brown. The oval seeds are about a quarter inch long. One side of the seed is smooth, while the other has ribbed edges and narrow wings. One parsnip plant produces approximately 1,000 seeds that remain viable for up to four years (Cornell Weed Identification, n.d.).

Look-Alike Plants

Golden alexander has similar flowers but is usually less than 30 inches tall (Cornell Weed Identification, n.d.). Also, its leaves have consistently toothed margins.

The giant hogweed has flat-topped flowers similar to parsnip flowers, but they are white instead of yellow. It has hairy stems with purple spots.

Wholesome Goodness

Parsnips are high in carbohydrates from fiber and natural sugars. They are low in fat and contain protein and vitamins C and E. In addition, they are exceptionally high in potassium, with one serving providing 10% of your daily recommended intake (White, 2022).

Minerals present include magnesium, calcium, iron, folate, and chlorine.

Filling Your Basket

The roots are the edible parts of wild parsnips. The best time to harvest them is in fall and winter when the plants are in the basal rosette stage. Remember that because wild parsnips grow according to the terrain, they will not always have uniform roots.

Forest to Table

Cook and eat wild parsnips as you would cultivated ones. Peel them before cooking. The core and rind may be denser than cultivated parsnips. Sometimes they taste a little spicy, but the spiciness fades after cooking.

PLANTAIN

THE HERB, NOT THE BANANA

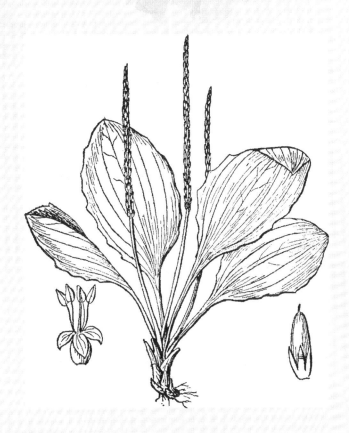

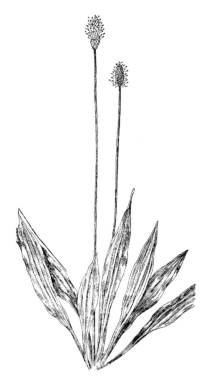

What's in a Name?

Plant Family: Plantaginaceae

Botanical Names and Common Names:

- *Plantago major* (greater plantain)
- *Plantago rugelii* (Rugel's plantain)
- *Plantago lanceolata* (lesser plantain)

The name plantain is of Old French origin and derived from Latin. *Planta* means the sole of the foot and refers to the plant's flat leaves.

https://bit.ly/
Plantain_31EWP

Did You Know?

Common plantain—or "plantain grass" abounds throughout Europe and North America. Plantain was found in the stomachs of mummified bog men, whose remains date back to the third and fifth centuries A.D. In the 11th century, plantain was recommended as a beneficial roadside herb (Weed Science Society of America, n.d.). Chaucer and Shakespeare both mentioned plantain in their literature.

The plant grows in over 50 countries and is considered a weed despite being edible and having medicinal properties (Weed Science Society of America, n.d.). It was dubbed "white man's foot" in colonial times because it appeared wherever Europeans settled. Puritans first brought plantain to New England.

Three species of plantain now grow in North America. Plantain loves the sun and prefers disturbed ground. You might find it in your lawn or along your driveway, although it thrives in rich, moist soil and is more likely to be found in orchards, nurseries, cultivated fields, and wastelands. Rugel's plantain, found in the eastern U.S., is thought to be a perennial native.

Plant Description

Plantain is a ground-hugging, herbaceous perennial with abundant, broad, round leaves. This plant possesses characteristics that have enabled it to spread globally and flourish nearly anywhere. Besides having a tough taproot, plantain reproduces prolifically. One plant sometimes produces as many as 14,000 seeds, which may be viable for as long as 60 years (MISIN, 2021). Plantain also reproduces vegetatively.

Leaves grow in a rosette 6–12 inches in diameter from the base of the plant and have prominent, parallel veins (MISIN, 2021). Leaf edges are smooth or slightly toothed. Mature leaves are thick and leathery. Greater plantain and Rugel's plantain have wide, oval leaves, but the latter can be distinguished by its purplish leaf stalks. The lesser plantain has narrow leaves that can be from a few inches to a foot long but are rarely wider than an inch (Meredith, 2015).

Flowers and seed heads emerge from the center of the rosette on long, leafless stalks 5–15 inches tall (MISIN, 2021). The seed heads of greater and Rugel's plantain cover most of their stalks, starting out as green seeds that are shaped like grains of rice and turn black or brown when ripe. Lesser plantain bears 1–2 inch seed heads with tiny white flowers (Meredith, 2015).

Plantain fruits consist of egg-shaped capsules less than 0.25 inches long, split across the middle into two equal segments containing 6–20 brown, glossy seeds (MISIN, 2021).

Look-Alike Plants

Hostas, or plantain lilies, look similar to plantain. Their leaves and shoots are also edible.

Wholesome Goodness

All three North American varieties of common plantain are nutritious, containing calcium, iron, magnesium, fiber, fat, protein, sodium, zinc, tannin, mucilage, and vitamins A, B, C, and K. The tiny seeds are high in protein.

For centuries, plantain has been used as a general herbal remedy and for treating specific ailments such as eye inflammation and open wounds. Its leaves contain soothing, mucilaginous fluid. Southern Europeans placed leaf poultices on scorpion stings and snake bites.

Filling Your Basket

Harvest greater plantain in spring and summer, and lesser plantain until the fall. In warmer climates, it is sometimes possible to gather the plant all year.

Young leaves are ideal for eating, as older leaves become tough and fibrous.

The tiny seeds can be harvested once they've turned brown or black.

Since plantain is an invasive plant, you can harvest it to your heart's content. In fact, the more plantain you remove, the happier your farming and gardening friends will be. Just check to ensure the plants you want to harvest have not been sprayed with herbicides or pesticides.

Forest to Table

Young plantain leaves have an earthy, slightly bitter flavor. Use them in soups and stews, as you would other dark, leafy greens. Substitute plantain for kale in recipes. Fry larger leaves to make vegetable crisps.

Seeds can be added to bread, muffins, and other savory baked goods.

PURSLANE

THE WONDERFUL, WORLDWIDE WEED

What's In a Name?

Plant Family: Portulacaceae

Botanical Name: *Portulaca oleracea*

Common Names: Common purslane, portulaca

Portulaca is derived from Latin and refers to the purging nature of some species. *Oleracea* is a Latin word meaning "cultivation" or "suitable for food."

https://bit.ly/ Purslane_31EWP

Did You Know?

There is a good chance this summer "weed" grows in your garden, in which case you can harvest it without traveling! Purslane has so many nutrients it could qualify as a superfood, so don't discard it when tidying up your yard. Purslane also colonizes open, sunny areas like cultivated fields, eroded slopes, roadsides, sidewalk cracks, disturbed soil, vacant lots, and wastelands.

No one is certain where purslane came from, although it is naturalized worldwide. It is a succulent plant, and one theory is that it may have originated in the deserts of North Africa. It was eaten over 2,000 years ago by the ancient Romans, Greeks, and Egyptians (FoodPrint, 2022).

Indigenous Americans used purslane medicinally and as a potherb. The plant could also have arrived with Indian immigrants who brought it to North America as a cooking ingredient. It occurs in the lower 48 U.S. states, southern Canada, and Hawaii.

Purslane is cultivated in southern Europe, the Mediterranean countries, and Asia as a potherb and salad ingredient. It is a valuable famine food. Gandhi famously said that purslane was one of his favorite foods.

Plant Description

Purslane is a succulent annual with a low spreading growth habit. It is fleshy with thick, reddish stems that spread into dense mats about 20 inches across (Four Season Foraging, 2018).

Leaves are succulent, spoon-shaped, and alternately arranged on the stem. They are about a half-inch wide and two-thirds inch long, with their broadest point above the middle (Four Season Foraging, 2018). They are smooth and green and may have a reddish tint near the edges.

Flowers are yellow and grow either singly or in terminal clusters. When fully open, each flower is about a quarter inch across with five petals, two green sepals, numerous yellow stamens, and several pistils grouped in the center of the flower (Stephenson, 2021). Flowers open for a few hours on bright, sunny mornings.

Seed capsules replace the flowers in fall and split down the middle to reveal numerous tiny black seeds.

Look-Alike Plants

The hairy-stemmed spurge looks just like purslane but is **highly poisonous. Be very sure that the plant you are harvesting is purslane and not this dangerous look-alike.** They are also sprawling plants with reddish coloring and have a similar range to purslane. The best and foolproof way to distinguish between spurge and purslane is that spurge leaves and stems exude a white milky sap when broken, torn, or cut. If you break the stem and no white liquid seeps out, you can be sure that you have found purslane. Also, spurge leaves are thin and flat, not succulent. Sometimes the leaves and stems of spurge are hairy, while purslane is not.

Wholesome Goodness

Purslane is a nutritional powerhouse, and it's no surprise to see it at farmers' markets or on restaurant menus. Purslane has seven times the beta-carotene of carrots, six times more vitamin E than spinach, and 14 times the omega-3 fatty acids of fish (Longacre, 2022). It also has significant amounts of vitamins A and C, calcium, magnesium, iron, potassium, and antioxidants.

This antibacterial plant is valued for natural medicine. It may relieve numerous ailments and medical conditions and boost immunity.

Important Note: Do not use purslane medicinally if you are pregnant or breastfeeding. It is not recommended for those with digestive complaints.

Filling Your Basket

The leaves, stems, and flowerheads are all edible. The plant tastes best when young, small, and close to the ground. Bigger purslane is also edible and easier to pick. Use scissors to cut off the soft leaves and stems.

Purslane flowers for about 1–2 months in midsummer to early fall (Stephenson, 2021). Harvest the flowers with scissors or by hand.

Wash the greens and flowers thoroughly before preparing and eating.

Forest to Table

Raw purslane is crunchy and tart, giving a lemony tang to salads. Cooking causes the tartness to dissipate, leaving it with a flavor resembling okra and spinach.

Cut off the roots and wash the stems and leaves carefully to remove all the dirt. Toss it into salads or add it to soups and omelets. Steam it briefly, add a little butter, and eat it as a vegetable. It goes well with cucumbers and other salad greens. Juice it or add it to smoothies.

Purslane can be wrapped in a paper towel or put into a plastic bag and refrigerated for a few days.

RED CURRANTS

THE FUCHSIA FLOWERS

RED CURRANTS

What's in a Name?

Family Name: Grossulariaceae
Botanical Name: *Ribes sanguineum*
Common Name: Red currant

The first part of the name is a corruption of an Arabic word, *rebus*, used for rhubarb, possibly on account of the tart flavor of the berries. The Romans later changed it to *ribes*. The species name derives from the Latin *sanguis*, meaning "blood," referring to the plant's floral splendor.

*https://bit.ly/
RedCurrantFlowers_31EWP*

Did You Know?

Red currants are stunningly beautiful shrubs, bearing heavy bunches of fuchsia-pink flowers in spring and summer and red berries in late summer and fall. They are native to North America and found mainly in the western U.S. and British Columbia. A similar species, Ribes americanum, commonly called wild black currants or American black currants, grows east of the Rocky Mountains all the way to the Atlantic coast, as far south as Virginia, Kentucky, Missouri, and Nebraska. The flowers and leaves of both red and black currants are delicious, although the berries are rather tart.

https://bit.ly/3DCCWS9

The natural beauty of red currant plants makes them prized garden ornamentals. Nurseries now stock several cultivars. Wild plants love the shade and are often found in Douglas fir forests. Red currants grow from sea level, at the coast, to elevations of up to 6,000 feet (Holmes, n.d.). Many types of wildlife, especially hummingbirds and various species of butterflies and moths, depend on these plants.

Moose and elk sometimes browse its leaves, songbirds nest in its branches, and birds and small mammals eat its berries. A red dye may be obtained from the fruit, while the leaves yield a yellow dye.

Plant Description

Red currants are deciduous shrubs with multiple stems that grow in clumps. They reach heights of 3–9.8 feet (Chris, 2021). Although they grow quickly and vigorously, the roots are light, thin, and easily damaged. The roots start off as taproots that later branch. Reproduction happens both by seed and root suckers.

Leaves are folded when they emerge, later becoming palmate with 3–5 lobes. They have toothed edges and are wider than they are long, measuring about 1–2 inches in length (Chris, 2021). They resemble black currant leaves and have fine hairs underneath. Mature leaves are dull green. When crushed, they release a fruity aromatic scent.

Flowers are the star of the show, buds appearing simultaneously with the leaves. Clusters of gorgeous fuchsia-pink flowers dangle from drooping stalks. Each flower has five petals and 18–24 flowers per cluster (Chris, 2021).

Fruits are round, dark purple, smooth-skinned berries, 2.4–4 inches in diameter (Holmes, n.d.). Each contains 3–10 minute bony seeds (Health Benefits Times, 2017).

Look-Alike Plants

Other currants look similar to red currants. They are also edible and bear small, greenish flowers.

Wholesome Goodness

Red currants contain iron, fiber, and potassium and are an excellent source of antioxidants and vitamins B and C. In addition, they are low in calories, so, great to eat if you are watching your weight.

Medicinally, red currants relieve various ailments, including eczema and acne. The fruit can even be used as a face mask to freshen the skin.

Filling Your Basket

The leaves, flowers, and fruit can all be eaten. Harvest the leaves in early spring by simply pinching them off the plant and discarding the leaf stalks. When the flowers bloom, between February and April, pinch or cut off the flower clusters with scissors.

Pick the berries with your fingers. Grab the T-shaped stalks to harvest multiple berries. They will easily separate from the stems when ripe.

Forest to Table

Eat the leaves and flowers raw, scattered on salads and puddings. The flowers have a delicious, fruity, floral flavor. Make syrups and cordials with them. Add them to vinegar to flavor savory foods. Flowers can be dried but do lose some of their flavor.

The fruits are not as sweet as black currants; some people find them quite tart. They are best sweetened, so use them in jams, jellies, preserves, pie fillings, and other desserts. Eat them fresh, with custard or sweet cream.

SHEEP SORREL

THE TENDER, TANGY TREAT

What's In a Name?

Plant Family: Polygonaceae

Botanical Name: *Rumex acetosella*

Common Names: Sheep sorrel, red sorrel, sour weed, field sorrel, French sorrel, dog-eared sorrel

The name sorrel comes from an old French word, *surelle*, meaning "sour."

Did You Know?

Sheep sorrel belongs to the buckwheat family. It originated in Eurasia and is naturalized in North America. It is a leafy green, cultivated in many countries as an herb and vegetable. It is regarded as a weed in the

https://bit.ly/ SheepSorrel_31EWP

U.S., although it has been eaten for hundreds of years. Indigenous Americans ate the whole plant and added it to meat dishes and bread. The Irish used it in soups, while the French added it to salads.

As a matter of interest, sheep sorrel can also be used as a general household cleaner. Use the juice to bleach and remove rust, mold, and ink from linen, wicker, and silverware.

The plant is a weed found in woodlands, grasslands, prairies, meadows, pastures, old fields, and disturbed areas. It grows as a rosette in the first year and then develops

https://bit.ly/ SheepSorrel2_31EWP

reddish, upright stems between 4–12 inches tall (Stephenson, 2021). It is often found near blueberries.

Cautions

Like spinach and other dark leafy greens, sheep sorrel contains oxalic acid, which may be detrimental if eaten in large quantities. Cooking does seem to moderate it, however.

Sheep sorrel should not be used medicinally by those prone to kidney stones because it could aggravate arthritis, rheumatism, endometriosis, and gout.

Children and pregnant or breastfeeding women should avoid it.

Plant Description

Sheep sorrel is a perennial. It initially consists of a clump of arrow-shaped leaves joined underground by the roots. In spring, each rosette sends up a reddish flower stem. The stems are slightly ridged and succulent. Plants grow in patches because of their creeping root systems. The whole plant tends to be reddish to brown in color.

Leaves are hairless, arranged alternately on the stem (one per node), and vary in size. Lower leaves have long leaf stalks, sometimes with a pair of slender lobes at the bottom of the blade. The middle leaves nearly always have a lateral lobe on either side, while the uppermost leaves are stalkless. The lobes sparkle in the sun.

Flowers are small and clustered in whorls on a branching inflorescence. This plant is unisexual, meaning that all the flowers on a plant are either male or female. Female flowers tend to be greenish, while male ones are yellowish. They bloom from May to July.

Fruits develop as the flowers fade. They are red and contain a single seed. Fruits later form a seed head reminiscent of a related plant, broad-leaved dock.

Look-Alike Plants

The leaves closely resemble field bindweed, although this sprawling plant grows along the ground and bears white flowers. Sorrel grows as a rosette and has tiny greenish or yellowish flowers. If unsure, a quick nibble will verify that you are indeed harvesting sorrel.

Wholesome Goodness

Sheep sorrel leaves are low in fat and have plenty of fiber and as much as 3 grams of protein per cup (Frey, 2022). One cup contains more vitamin A and vitamin C than the daily recommended allowance, in addition to folate, small amounts of vitamin B6, and antioxidants. The plant is particularly rich in potassium, phosphorus, magnesium, and calcium, together with iron, zinc, copper, sodium, and other essential nutrients.

Sheep sorrel is an astringent, anthelmintic, cooling, blood-cleansing, and detoxifying herb. It is often taken as a spring tonic tea. It was an ingredient in "essiac tea," an Indigenous American herbal infusion also containing burdock, Chinese rhubarb, and slippery elm. This tea was widely used in the 19th century and, among other things, was considered a remedy for cancer (Swart, 2022).

Filling Your Basket

The leaves are edible, while the whole plant can be used medicinally. Harvest the leaves in early spring until midsummer, before the plant flowers, to obtain the best flavors. They are less bitter in early spring. Look for green, healthy leaves with no brown spots. Cut them off the plants with scissors. If there is a large patch of plants, harvest small amounts from each one.

For medicinal use, sorrel root can be harvested in the fall.

Forest to Table

Sheep sorrel has a lemony, tangy, or tart flavor, so a little will go a long way. Cook it like spinach and change the water once to eliminate the bitterness and much of the oxalic acid. Puree the leaves and use them in baked fish, or add them to homemade mayonnaise and pancake batter. Use cooked leaves in soups, meat and chicken casseroles, soft cheese dips, and gravies. Sorrel goes well with pork.

The leaves act as a thickener in soups and stews. Sheep sorrel tenderizes meat when added to marinades or used to wrap meat.

Eat the seeds raw or cooked, grind them into a powder for flour, or add them to savory baked goods.

SIBERIAN ELM

THE TREE WITH GROOVY BARK

What's In A Name?

Plant Family: Ulmaceae

Botanical Name: *Ulmus pumila*

Common Names: Siberian elm, Chinese elm

Ulmus, the ancient Roman name for this tree, means "elm," while pumila means "dwarf."

Did You Know?

https://bit.ly/ SiberianElm_31EWP

This elm tree actually originated in Siberia and is also native to parts of China, Manchuria, and Korea. In the 1860s, it was imported to the U.S. as an ornamental. It was extensively planted because it is a hardwood resistant to drought and cold. Planted on farmlands in the 1960s as a windbreak and to control erosion, it spread across North America (North Dakota Department of Agriculture, n.d.). The young leaves, inner bark, and seeds are all edible.

A coarse cloth can be made from the inner bark. The tree twists as it grows, which makes the wood very hard to split for firewood. However, this made it ideal for making wagon wheel hubs, preventing them from splitting when oak spokes were driven into them.

Siberian elms thrive in fertile, well-drained soil but also tolerate adverse conditions. They grow in moist places along streams and roadsides, in pastures and grasslands. They germinate readily and grow quickly, with seedlings establishing in early spring.

Plant Description

Siberian elms are medium trees with drooping branches and rounded canopies. They reach heights of 50–70 feet (North Dakota Department of Agriculture, n.d.). The bark is dark gray and becomes deeply grooved with long, flat, interlaced ridges. Stems, which may be slightly hairy, are slender, brittle, and very light gray or grayish-green.

Leaves are simple, arranged alternately on the stem, elliptical, smooth, and slightly toothed. They are between half and two-and-a-half inches long (North Dakota Department of Agriculture, n.d.). The dark green leaves have paler undersides and are almost hairless.

Flowers are greenish with no petals and occur in small, compact clusters of 2–5 blossoms along the twigs (North Dakota Department of Agriculture, n.d.). The flower stalks are either short or absent. Flowers appear before the leaves or simultaneously.

Fruits, called samaras, are winged, smooth, circular, or obovate. The wings are light brown and notched at the tip. The fruits are a quarter to half an inch long, wrinkled, and hang in clusters (Missouri Department of Conservation, n.d.). Each contains a single seed.

Look-Alike Plants

Differences in the leaves distinguish the American elm from the Siberian elm. The former has much longer leaves with asymmetrical leaf bases and leaf margins with double teeth. On the other hand, Siberian elm tree leaves have entire or single-toothed margins.

Wholesome Goodness

Siberian elm leaves are diuretic. Stem bark is demulcent and diuretic. It can be used as a tea for upset stomachs and digestive ailments.

Filling Your Basket

Siberian elms are only in season for two weeks to a month. So be on the lookout to ensure you don't miss out on this springtime foraging opportunity (Bergo, 2022).

The leaves, inner bark, and samaras are all edible. The main harvest is the fruits available in April or May. Simply pick them off the tree.

To find fruits you can reach, walk along the edges of woods, sunny fields, and trails. Trees growing in these locations also get more sun and will have more fruits. Choose light-green, tender samaras in clusters. Avoid those with tough, papery wings unless you want to harvest the seeds. Remember to bring a container, preferably one you can attach to your belt to increase your harvesting speed.

If you harvest samaras after they have dried, you can still eat the seeds. Simply rub the dry, papery wings off the seeds, and you're in business.

Pinch or pick young leaves off the tree in spring. Harvest the inner bark any time of year, taking care not to ringbark the tree.

Forest to Table

Samaras are small, so pick plenty. Prepare them by chilling them in a paper bag in the refrigerator before eating or cooking.

Siberian elm samaras can be eaten raw in salads, although they are particularly delicious when cooked. Add them to soups at the last minute and watch the color change. Sauté with olive oil or butter. Toast them and eat them as a delicious snack.

The dried seeds taste a little like sunflower seeds, but the dry wings need to be winnowed to enjoy them. Grind the winnowed seeds and add to flour for baking bread and other goodies.

The inner bark can be ground and added to cereal flours or used as a thickener for soups and stews.

WILD GARLIC

THE PLANT WITH A TELLTALE AROMA

What's in a Name?

Family Name: Liliaceae
Botanical Name: *Allium vineale*
Common Names: Wild garlic, crow garlic, onion grass, stag's garlic, field garlic, wild onion

Did You Know?

Native to Europe, North Africa, and the Middle East, garlic has become naturalized worldwide. The ancient Chinese cultivated it and first recorded its medicinal benefits 8,000 years ago (Food4Life Market, 2021). Egyptian and Indian cultures also used garlic. Presently, the only genuinely wild garlic is found in central Asia, where it originated.

*https://bit.ly/
WildGarlic_31EWP*

Wild garlic is related to other plants from the *Allium* genus: onions, chives, and shallots. Despite being an important food and medicinal plant, it is considered a noxious weed in North America because it is reproduces aggressively and is difficult to eradicate.

Wild garlic is a lawn weed that prefers disturbed areas with moist soil, and full sun to partial shade. You'll find it along roadsides and in thickets, meadows, and woodlands. Because the leaves look similar to grass leaf blades, wild garlic can be difficult to find until you smell the unmistakable odor. The plants form colonies, so you'll probably find several in one location.

Plant Description

Wild garlic is an herbaceous perennial that grows to heights of 1–3 feet (N.C. State Extension, n.d.). The long, rounded central stem is unbranched and hairless. The root is a bulb with secondary bulblets. Bulblets produced by the mother plant enable vegetative repro- duction.

Leaves are small, alternate, and on the lower end of the stem. They are linear, sword-shaped, smooth, fragile, and hollow towards the inside of the base. Leaves are rounded and become slightly flattened where they wrap around the stem. They have a strong, garlicky aroma.

Flowers are rare. When they form, it is on the end of the stem, often above aerial bulblets. The mature inflorescence is about 2–3 inches across. During the early stages, the entire flower may be covered by a membrane that eventually splits open to release the bulblets and the flower. The bulblets are green to dark red, about half an inch long, and oblong with a long tail. The flowers are green, white, or mauve, consisting of six tepals that are erect or slightly spreading (Illinois Wildflowers, n.d.).

Several seeds grow inside a capsule and are small and black.

Look-Alike Plants

Wild garlic is similar to cultivated garlic, but the former's aerial bulblets have much longer green tails and a more striking appearance. Its leaves are also hollow at the base.

Wholesome Goodness

Wild garlic contains vitamins A and C, potassium, manganese, calcium, and selenium. It also has immune-boosting, antimicrobial, and anti-inflammatory properties.

Filling Your Basket

The leaves, flowers, and bulbs are all edible. Wild garlic prefers cooler temperatures, so it is usually available in spring and early summer. After that, plants die back until fall, which is wonderful because it results in two harvesting seasons. Wild garlic flowers from late spring to early summer for about 2–3 weeks (Illinois Wildflowers, n.d.).

Forest to Table

Wild garlic can be used like spring onions, cultivated garlic, or onions. Use young, tender leaves as a substitute for chives in recipes and savory foods. Chop fresh leaves for salads, dressings, and marinades, or make flavored butter, oil, and vinegar. You can add chopped bulblets to almost any raw or cooked dish. The leaves and bulblets can be pickled and preserved, or the leaves can be dried and stored for when fresh wild garlic is unavailable. Bulbs wrapped in plastic will keep in the refrigerator for about a week.

CONCLUSION

Foraging for edible wild plants is a wonderful activity that will enable you to utilize many delicious and nutritious food sources. It will also bring you back to nature and help you walk a path toward a more sustainable life. You will probably also connect with enthusiastic, like-minded people on similar journeys.

The world is changing rapidly, and everyone will need to be more self-reliant in the future. Harvesting some of your own food will increase your autonomy and decrease your vulnerability to global supply chains, giant food corporations, potential food shortages, and trade disruptions. In addition, foraging could be a way to minimize your reliance on third parties to provide all your needs. Perhaps it will even be the first step in your adventure of living off the land, if that is one of your goals or dreams.

Whether or not you consider yourself a foodie, becoming a forager will inspire you to take advantage of delicious, freshly harvested wild greens, vegetables, roots, fruit, and seeds. You might surprise yourself with the extra nutrients and unique flavor profiles added to your meals.

Foraging is an enriching and educational experience through which you will learn more about the natural world, track seasonal changes, and watch the creatures that use the same plants as you do. You embark on a lifelong adventure of becoming acquainted with hundreds or even thousands of plants and trees that can be used as food or medicine. You will probably spend countless hours, days, and even months roaming woods and fields, lakeshores and marshes, rocky outcroppings, and desert fringes in your quest for wild edibles.

In this book, you have already learned about 31 species of edible wild plants that grow across North America. Now it's time to turn that knowledge into action and discover these plants outdoors! With the foundation of everything you have learned through reading plant descriptions and looking at illustrations, you are ready to get out there and begin foraging.

So, what are you waiting for? Find a basket or bag, some harvesting tools, and a friend or family member. Then, get out into nature and look for some of these wild plants to identify and eat. Be safe, and enjoy the adventure!

ONE LAST INVITATION!

It was wonderful to have you join me on this path of learning about 31 edible wild plants. Thanks for coming along!

You now have information that you didn't have before. You're ready to head out into nature with confidence that you can identify edible wild plants safely and successfully.

But there are beginning foragers out there who are still worried about how to tell the edible wild plants apart from the dangerous ones, or who simply feel overwhelmed by all there is to learn about foraging. They are looking for answers but don't know where to go.

Would you please leave a quick review for this book to help them get the answers that you have discovered?

It won't cost you a thing, just a couple minutes of your time. This is not an essay question or school assignment, and doesn't need to be long or detailed.

A one-sentence honest review stating something about the book that set it apart or was helpful is enough. You can make a difference in helping other people succeed on their path of foraging and becoming more self-sufficient.

Thank you for caring enough to leave a review here:

https://bit.ly/review31ediblewildplantsbook

Or scan this QR code

REFERENCES

Adamant, A. (2019a, March 16). *Foraging Yellow dock (curly dock, and other Rumex sp.).* Practical Self Reliance. https://practicalselfreliance.com/foraging-yellow-dock-curly-dock-rumex-sp/

Adamant, A. (2019b, December 23). *Foraging nannyberry (Viburnum lentago).* Practical Self Reliance. https://practicalselfreliance.com/nannyberry-viburnum-lentago/

Aggie Horticulture. (n.d.). *Two Mediterranean root crops.* Archives Aggie Horticulture. Retrieved July 14, 2022, from https://aggie-horticulture.tamu.edu/archives/parsons/publications/vegetabletravels/parsnip.html

Anwiksha. (2011, October 4). *Daylily (Hemerocallis)—Nutrition facts, benefits, uses, pictures.* Only Foods. https://www.onlyfoods.net/daylily-hemerocallis.html

Austin, A. (2005, November). *Black locust.* Bellarmine. https://www.bellarmine.edu/faculty/drobinson/blacklocust.asp#:~:text=The%20Black%20Locust%20is%20native

Baessler, L. (n.d.). *What to do with elderberry flowers.* Gardening Know How. Retrieved July 14, 2022, from https://www.gardeningknowhow.com/edible/fruits/elderberry/what-to-do-with-elderflowers.htm

Baillargeon, Z. (2020, September 10). *A beginner's guide to foraging.* The Manual. https://www.themanual.com/food-and-drink/beginners-guide-to-foraging/

Banker, P. (2020, June 3). *History's editable "weed": Lambs quarters.* New York Almanac. https://www.newyorkalmanack.com/2020/06/historys-editable-weed-lambs-quarters/

Begum, T. (2021, May 19). *What is mass extinction and are we facing a sixth one?* Natural History Museum, London. https://www.nhm.ac.uk/discover/what-is-mass-extinction-and-are-we-facing-a-sixth-one.html

Ben-Erik Van Wyk, & Gericke, N. (2000). *People's plants: A guide to useful plants of Southern Africa.* Briza Publications.

Berardi, D. J. (n.d.). *Fiddleheads recipe & nutrition—Precision Nutrition's Encyclopedia of Food.* Precision Nutrition. Retrieved July 14, 2022, from https://www.precisionnutrition.com/encyclopedia/food/fiddleheads#:~:text=Nutrition%20Info

Bergo, A. (2022, May 14). *Elm samaras.* Forager Chef. https://foragerchef.com/elm-samaras/

Berrie, T. and B. (2020). *Arrowhead.* Our Tiny Homestead. https://www.ourtinyhomestead.com/arrowhead.html

Bowness, K. (n.d.). *Foraging guide: Flowering currant UK foraging.* Foraging Course Site. Retrieved July 14, 2022, from https://www.foragingcoursecompany.co.uk/foraging-guide-flowering-currant

Burnham, R. J. (2015, July 28). *Lonicera sempervirens Climbers.* Climbers. https://climbers.lsa.umich.edu/?p=197

Chandran, R. (2020, June). *Common chickweed*. West Virginia Extension. https://exten sion.wvu.edu/lawn-gardening-pests/weeds/common-chickweed#:~:text=Chick-weed%20likely%20got%20its%20name

Chapman, J. L., & Reiss, M. (1999). *Ecology : Principles and applications*. Cambridge University Press.

Chris. (2021, March 19). *Foraging the flowering currant (Ribes sanguineum) Grossulariaceae family*. Wild Plant Guides. https://wildplantguides.com/2021/03/19/foraging-flower-ing-currant-ribes-sanguineum/

Codekas, C. (2020a, July 28). *Foraging plantain: Identification and uses*. Grow Forage Cook Ferment. https://www.growforagecookferment.com/plantain-natures-band-aid/

Codekas, C. (2020b, August 22). *Foraging for elderberries & elderflowers: identification, look-alikes, & uses*. Grow Forage Cook Ferment. https://www.growforagecookfer-ment.com/foraging-for-elderberries/

Contributors, W. E. (2020, September 17). *Parsnip: Health benefits, nutrition, and uses*. WebMD. https://www.webmd.com/diet/health-benefits-parsnip#:~:text=Along%20with%20vitamin%20C%2C%20parsnips

Cornell Botanic Gardens. (n.d.). *Marsh marigold*. Cornell Botanic Gardens. https://cornell botanicgardens.org/plant/marsh-marigold/

Cornell Weed Identification. (n.d.). *Wild Parsnip*. Cornell University. Retrieved July 14, 2022, from https://blogs.cornell.edu/weedid/wild-parsnip/

Deane, G. (2019, May 4). *Basswood tree, linden, lime tree*. Eat the Weeds and Other Things, Too. https://www.eattheweeds.com/basswood-tree-linden-lime-tree/

Deanne, G. (2011, August 31). *Chinese elm take out*. Eat the Weeds and Other Things, Too. https://www.eattheweeds.com/chinese-elm-a-tree-that-doesnt-go-dutch-2/#:~:text=The%20Siberian%20Elm%20is%20likewise

Department of Agriculture, Forestry and Fisheries. (2010). *Amaranthus production guideline*. Department of Agriculture Forestry and Fisheries. https://www.nda.a-gric.za/docs/brochures/amaranthus.pdf

Dodrill, T. (2019, July 25). *Chicory: how to find and use this powerful plant*. Survival Sulli-van. https://www.survivalsullivan.com/chicory/#Chicory_Plant_History

Dyer, M. H. (2017a, April 20). *History of edible burdock plants*. Gardening Know How. https://blog.gardeningknowhow.com/tbt/history-edible-burdock-plants/

Dyer, M. H. (2017b, June 1). *History of dandelion plants*. Gardening Know How. https://blog.gardeningknowhow.com/tbt/dandelion-plant-history-facts/

Ellis, M. E. (2019, March 14). *History of clover plants*. Gardening Know How. https://blog.-gardeningknowhow.com/tbt/history-of-clover-plants/

Elm bark. (2021, June 11). RxList. https://www.rxlist.com/elm_bark/supplements.htm

Encyclopedia.com. (2019). *Sheep sorrel*. Encyclopedia.com. https://www.encyclopedia.-com/medicine/encyclopedias-almanacs-transcripts-and-maps/sheep-sorrel

Encyclopedia Britannica. (n.d.-a). *Chickweed description, species, & facts*. Encyclopedia Britannica. Retrieved July 14, 2022, from https://www.britannica.com/plant/chickweed

Encyclopedia Britannica. (n.d.-b). *Elderberry description, species, & uses*. Encyclopedia Britannica. https://www.britannica.com/plant/elder-plant

English Stack Exchange. (n.d.). *Confusion surrounding etymology of "burdock."* English Language & Usage Stack Exchange. Retrieved July 14, 2022, from https://english.stackexchange.com/questions/549173/confusion-surrounding-etymology-of-burdock

Everett, W. (2021, October 29). *Foraging for brambleberries—Insteading.* Insteading. https://insteading.com/blog/foraging-for-brambleberries/

Ferment, G. F. C. (2015, May 31). *Foraging for cattails.* Grow Forage Cook Ferment. https://www.growforagecookferment.com/foraging-for-cattails/

Ferment, G. F. C. (2016, October 6). *Foraging for chicory.* Grow Forage Cook Ferment. https://www.growforagecookferment.com/foraging-for-chicory/

Fertig, W. (n.d.). *Arrowhead.* US Forest Service. Retrieved July 16, 2022, from https://www.fs.fed.us/wildflowers/plant-of-the-week/sagittaria_cuneata.shtml

Firdous, D. (2020, June 27). *Benefits of cattail and its side effects.* Lybrate. https://www.lybrate.com/topic/benefits-of-cattail-and-its-side-effects#:~:text=The%20health%20benefits%20of%20Cattail

Fire Effects Information System. (n.d.-a). *Robinia pseudoacacia.* US Forest Service. Retrieved July 14, 2022, from https://www.fs.fed.us/database/feis/plants/tree/robpse/all.html#:~:text=Native%20range%3A%20Black%20locust%20inhabits

Fire Effects Information System. (n.d.-b). *Tilia americana.* US Forest Service. Retrieved July 14, 2022, from https://www.fs.fed.us/database/feis/plants/tree/tilame/all.html#:~:text=SITE%20CHARACTERISTICS%3A%20American%20basswood%20is

Food4Life Market. (n.d.). *The history of garlic.* Food 4 Life Market. Retrieved July 14, 2022, from https://www.food4lifemarket.com/history-of-garlic

Four Seasons Foraging. (2018, July 24). *Purslane identification.* Four Season Foraging. https://www.fourseasonforaging.com/blog/2018/7/24/purslane-identification

Frey, M. (2011, January 13). *Why Sorrel might become your new favorite superfood.* Verywell Fit. https://www.verywellfit.com/sorrel-benefits-side-effects-and-preparations-4211503

Frits Van Oudtshoorn, & Van Wyk, E. (1999). *Guide to grasses of Southern Africa.* Briza Publications.

Fruits Info. (2022). *Honeysuckle fruit nutrition facts—honeysuckle fruit.* Health Benefits. https://www.fruitsinfo.com/honeysuckle.php

Fuller, D. (n.d.). Bulletin #2540, *Ostrich fern fiddleheads, Matteuccia struthiopteris.* Cooperative Extension Publications. Retrieved July 14, 2022, from https://extension.umaine.edu/publications/2540e/#:~:text=Fiddleheads%20are%20harvested%20in%20the

Gardening Channel. (2011, December 19). *Ostrich fern fiddleheads: How to identify and cook.* Gardening Channel. https://www.gardeningchannel.com/ostrich-fern-fiddleheads-how-to-identify-and-cook/

Gardening, U. (2022, May 12). *Foraging black locust flowers.* Unruly Gardening. https://unrulygardening.com/foraging-black-locust-flowers/

Giani, P. (2004). *Antioxidant activity and nutritional values in fruits of Viburnum lentago.* ProQuest. https://www.proquest.com/openview/19781eaa56b5dd6245d26b495b0248ef/1?pq-origsite=gscholar&cbl=18750&diss=y

Grant, A. (2018, July 12). *History of blackberries.* Gardening Know How. https://blog.gardeningknowhow.com/tbt/history-of-blackberries/

Greene, W. (2015, May 4). *Black locust: The tree on which the US was built.* Live Science. https://www.livescience.com/50732-black-locust-tree-shaped-the-united-states.html

Haddock, B. (2012, May 12). *Sheep sorrel—edible wild plant—how to find, identify, prepare, and other uses for survival.* Wilderness Arena Survival. https://www.wildernessarena.com/food-water-shelter/food-food-water-shelter/food-procurement/edible-wild-plants/sheep-sorrel

HarFord, R. (2017, July 21). *Dandelion—a foraging guide to its food, medicine and other uses.* Eatweeds. https://www.eatweeds.co.uk/dandelion-taraxacum-officinale

Harford, R. (2018, May 18). *Blackberry—a foraging guide to its food, medicine and other uses.* Eatweeds. https://www.eatweeds.co.uk/bramble-blackberry-rubus-fruticosus

Harford, R. (2019, April 30). *Plantain—a foraging guide to its food, medicine and other uses.* Eatweeds. https://www.eatweeds.co.uk/ribwort-and-greater-plantain-plantago-spp

Harris, L. (2022, May 19). *A beginner's guide to foraging.* EcoWatch. https://www.ecowatch.com/foraging-101.html

Harris, T. (2022, April 11). *Are consumers seeing a future of empty shelves?* SAP News Center. https://news.sap.com/2022/04/consumers-seeing-future-post-pandemic

Health Benefits Times. (2016a, May 16). *Arrowhead facts, health benefits and nutritional value.* Health Benefits Times. https://www.healthbenefitstimes.com/arrowhead/

Health Benefits Times. (2016b, June 22). *Lamb's quarters—Chenopodium album.* Health Benefits Times. https://www.healthbenefitstimes.com/lambs-quarters/

Health Benefits Times. (2017, June 7). *Redcurrant facts and health benefits.* Health Benefits Times. https://www.healthbenefitstimes.com/redcurrant/

Health Benefits Times. (2018, October 11). *Field penny-cress facts and health benefits.* Health Benefits Times. https://www.healthbenefitstimes.com/field-penny-cress/

Health Benefits Times. (2020, March 8). *Orange daylily facts and health benefits.* Health Benefits Times. https://www.healthbenefitstimes.com/orange-daylily/

Health Benefits Times. (2021a, January 4). *Nannyberry facts and health benefits.* Health Benefits Times. https://www.healthbenefitstimes.com/nannyberry/

Health Benefits Times. (2021b, May 7). *Black locust facts and health benefits.* Health Benefits Times. https://www.healthbenefitstimes.com/black-locust/

Health Hutt. (2019, September 15). *Elderberry's exciting history.* Health Hutt. https://the-healthhutt.com/elderberrys-exciting-history/

Henofthewood. (2013, May 28). *Foraging: Identifying & harvesting black locust.* The Foraged Foodie. https://foragedfoodie.blogspot.com/2013/05/foraging-identifying-harvesting-blackhtml

Holmes, R. (n.d.). *Red-flowering currant.* US Forest Service. https://www.fs.fed.us/wildflowers/plant-of-the-week/ribes_sanguineum.shtml

https://www.facebook.com/growforagecookferment. (2015, April 5). *Foraging for dandelions.* Grow Forage Cook Ferment. https://www.growforagecookferment.com/foraging-for-dandelions/

REFERENCES

Illinois Wildflowers. (n.d.-a). *Curly dock (Rumex crispus)*. Illinois Wildflowers. Retrieved July 14, 2022, from https://www.illinoiswildflowers.info/weeds/plants/curly_-dock.htm

Illinois Wildflowers. (n.d.-b). *Field garlic (Allium vineale)*. Illinois Wildflowers. Retrieved July 14, 2022, from https://www.illinoiswildflowers.info/weeds/plants/field_garlic.htm

Illinois Wildflowers. (n.d.-c). *Hog peanut (Amphicarpaea bracteata)*. Illinois Wildflowers. Retrieved July 14, 2022, from https://www.illinoiswildflowers.info/savanna/plants/hog_peanut.html#:~:text=Hog%20Peanut%20(Amphicarpaea%20bracteata)&text=Description%3A%20This%20vine%20is%20a

Inc, R. P. (2017, August 15). *Foraging for beginners: What you need to know before you start.* Rootwell. https://www.rootwell.com/blogs/foraging-beginners

Indigo Herbs. (n.d.). *Chickweed benefits.* Indigo Herbs. Retrieved July 14, 2022, from https://www.indigo-herbs.co.uk/natural-health-guide/benefits/chickweed

Invasive Species Center. (2022). *Japanese knotweed—profile and resources.* Invasive Species Centre. https://www.invasivespeciescentre.ca/invasive-species/meet-the-species/invasive-plants/japanese-knotweed/

Invasive Species Compendium. (2019). *Rumex crispus (curled dock).* CABI. https://www.cabi.org/isc/datasheet/48059

Izzy Cooking. (2020, September 18). *Edible purslane weeds and easy purslane recipe (+ health benefits).* IzzyCooking. https://izzycooking.com/purslane/

Japanese knotweed: Dreadable edible. (2011, November 9). Eat the Weeds and Other Things, Too. https://www.eattheweeds.com/japanese-knotweed-dreadable-edible/

Keeler, K. H. (2017, July 9). *A wandering botanist: Plant story—curly dock, uses and folklore.* A Wandering Botanist. https://khkeeler.blogspot.com/2017/07/plant-story-curly-dock-uses-and-folklore.html

Keeler, K. H. (2018, May 13). *A wandering botanist: Plant story—daylilies, from Asia, beautiful and not lilies.* A Wandering Botanist. https://khkeeler.blogspot.com/2018/05/plant-story-daylilies-from-asia.html#:~:text=Daylilies%20-came%20to%20the%20West%20from%20China

Khula Dhamma, South Africa. (2020). Naturalhomes. http://naturalhomes.org/timeline/khuladhamma.htm

Kokotkiewicz, A., Jaremicz, Z., & Luczkiewicz, M. (2010). Aronia plants: A review of traditional use, biological activities, and perspectives for modern medicine. *Journal of Medicinal Food, 13(2),* 255–269. https://doi.org/10.1089/jmf.2009.0062

Krohn, E. (2013, April 30). *Chickweed.* Wild Foods and Medicines. http://wildfoodsandmedicines.com/chickweed/#:~:text=When%20and%20How%20to%20Harvest

Lamattina, A & G. (2017, October 20). *A history of Parsnips.* A & G Lamattina & Sons Ltd. https://lamattina.com.au/2017/10/20/a-history-of-parsnips/

Lapcevic, K. (2016, June 15). *Using honeysuckle for food and medicine.* Homespun Seasonal Living. https://homespunseasonalliving.com/using-honeysuckle-for-food-and-medicine/

Larum, D. (n.d.). *Herbal use of chickweed plants.* Gardening Know How. Retrieved July 14, 2022, from https://www.gardeningknowhow.com/plant-problems/weeds/herbal-

use-of-chickweed-plants.
htm#:~:text=Chickweed%20flowers%20and%20leaves%20can

Lewis, N. (2004, November). *Curly dock*. Bellarmine. https://www.bellarmine.edu/faculty/drobinson/curlydock.asp#:~:text=Curly%20Dock%20is%20a%20species

Link, K. (n.d.). *Blackberries, raspberries, brambles*. FoodPrint. Retrieved July 14, 2022, from https://foodprint.org/real-food/brambles-aka-blackberries-raspberries-and-more/

Link, K. (2022). *Purslane*. FoodPrint. https://foodprint.org/real-food/purslane/#:https://foodprint.org/real-food/purslane/#:~:text=A%20fleshy%2C%20leafy%20green%2C%20purslane

Link, R. (2021, August 12). *Sorrel: Nutrients, benefits, downsides, and recipes*. Healthline. https://www.healthline.com/nutrition/sorrel-benefits

Longacre, C. (2022, June 5). *Purslane: Health benefits and recipes*. Almanac. https://www.almanac.com/purslane-health-benefits-and-recipes

Mahr, S. (n.d.). *Field pennycress, Thlaspi arvense*. Wisconsin Horticulture. https://hort.extension.wisc.edu/articles/field-pennycress-thlapsi-arvense/

Marler, B. (2019, March 5). *Publisher's platform: One year ago today—Tiger Brands polony linked to South Africa listeria outbreak*. Food Safety News. https://www.foodsafetynews.com/2019/03/publishers-platform-one-year-ago-today-tiger-brands-polony-linked-to-south-africa-listeria-outbreak/

Media, S., & Vill, L. (2006). *Common chickweed*. US Forest Service. https://www.invasive.org/weedcd/pdfs/wow/common-chickweed.pdf

Medicinal herbs: Siberian elm—Ulmus pumila. (n.d.). Natural Medicinal Herbs. Retrieved July 14, 2022, from http://www.naturalmedicinalherbs.net/herbs/u/ulmus-pumila=siberian-elm.php

Meredith, L. (2015, July 2). *Foraging plantain & recipe for plantain leaf chips*. Leda Meredith. https://ledameredith.com/foraging-plantain-leaves-for-food-and-medicine-no-not-that-plant/

Minnesota Department of Agriculture. (n.d.). *Japanese knotweed*. Minnesota Department of Agriculture. https://www.mda.state.mn.us/plants/pestmanagement/weedcontrol/noxiouslist/knotweed

Minnesota Wildflowers. (n.d.). *Amphicarpaea bracteata (American hog peanut)*. Minnesota Wildflowers. Retrieved July 14, 2022, from https://www.minnesotawildflowers.info/flower/american-hog-peanut

MISIN. (2020). *Japanese knotweed*. MISIN. http://www.misin.msu.edu/facts/detail/?id=25

MISIN. (2021). *Common plantain*. MISIN. https://www.misin.msu.edu/facts/detail/?project=misin&id=421&cname=Common+plantain

Missouri Department of Conservation. (n.d.). *Siberian elm—field guide*. Missouri Department of Conservation. Retrieved July 14, 2022, from https://mdc.mo.gov/discover-nature/field-guide/siberian-elm#:~:text=Siberian%20elm%20is%20a%20medium

Morgenstern, K. (2021, September 29). *Foraging: Evening primrose (Oenothera biennis)*. Sacred Earth. https://sacredearth.com/2021/09/29/foraging-evening-primrose-oenothera-biennis/

Moulton, M. (2022, February 10). *Edible ferns: Identifying, growing & harvesting fiddle-heads.* Rural Sprout. https://www.ruralsprout.com/fiddleheads/

Munteanu, N. (2021, October 2). *Finding magic in the basswood tree—foraging.* The Meaning of Water. https://themeaningofwater.com/2021/10/02/finding-magic-in-the-basswood-tree-foraging/

National Geographic Education. (2022). *The development of agriculture.* National Geographic Society. https://education.nationalgeographic.org/resource/development-agriculture

National Park Service. (2018, March 21). *Cattails.* National Park Service. https://www.nps.gov/miss/learn/nature/cattails.htm

NC State Extension. (n.d.-a). *Allium vineale (crow garlic, field garlic, onion grass, stag's garlic, wild garlic, wild onion).* North Carolina Extension Gardener Plant Toolbox. https://plants.ces.ncsu.edu/plants/allium-vineale/

NC State Extension. (n.d.-b). *Arctium minus (bardane, common burdock, lesser burdock).* North Carolina Extension Gardener Plant Toolbox. https://plants.ces.ncsu.edu/plants/arctium-minus/

NC State Extension. (n.d.-c). *Aronia arbutifolia (chokeberry, red chokeberry).* North Carolina Extension Gardener Plant Toolbox. https://plants.ces.ncsu.edu/plants/aronia-arbutifolia/

NC State Extension. (n.d.-d). *Hemerocallis (Day lilies, daylily, day lily).* North Carolina Extension Gardener Plant Toolbox. Retrieved July 14, 2022, from https://plants.ces.ncsu.edu/plants/hemerocallis/

NC State Extension. (n.d.-e). *Sambucus canadensis (American elder, American elderberry, common elderberry, elderberry).* North Carolina Extension Gardener Plant Toolbox. https://plants.ces.ncsu.edu/plants/sambucus-canadensis/

NC State Extension. (n.d.-f). *Stellaria media (birdweed, chickenwort, chickweed, common chickweed, starweed, starwort, winterweed).* North Carolina Extension Gardener Plant Toolbox. Retrieved July 14, 2022, from https://plants.ces.ncsu.edu/plants/stellaria-media/#:~:text=Stellaria%20media%2C%20or%20Chickweed%2C%20is

NC State Extension. (n.d.-g). *Taraxacum officinale (Dandelion, lion's tooth).* North Carolina Extension Gardener Plant Toolbox. https://plants.ces.ncsu.edu/plants/taraxacum-officinale/

NC State Extension. (n.d.-h). *Trifolium repens (clover, Dutch clover, ladino clover, purple Dutch clover, shamrock, white clover).* North Carolina Extension Gardener Plant Toolbox. https://plants.ces.ncsu.edu/plants/trifolium-repens/

New World Encyclopedia. (n.d.). *Clover.* New World Encyclopedia. https://www.newworldencyclopedia.org/entry/Clover

North Dakota Department of Agriculture. (n.d.). *Siberian elm (Ulmus pumila).* North Dakota Department of Agriculture. https://www.nd.gov/ndda/sites/default/files/legacy/resource/SIBERIANELM.pdf

Nutrition Authority. (2014, January 24). *Burdock is a nutritional, medicinal and an edible plant.* Nutrition Authority. https://nutritionauthority.com/uncategorized/new-ways-with-vegetables-burdock-root/

Office of Regulatory Affairs. (2019). *Recalls, market withdrawals, & safety alerts.* U.S. Food and Drug Administration. https://www.fda.gov/safety/recalls-market-withdrawals-safety-alerts

Oregon State University. (2019, January 29). *Cover crops. Species.* Forage Information System. https://forages.oregonstate.edu/oregon/topics/cover-crops/species

Parkin, S. (2018, March 4). *Has dopamine got us hooked on tech?* The Guardian. https://www.theguardian.com/technology/2018/mar/04/has-dopamine-got-us-hooked-on-tech-facebook-apps-addiction

Pennsylvania State University. (2016, August 9). *Home fruit plantings: Elderberries.* Penn State Extension. https://extension.psu.edu/home-fruit-plantings-elderberries#:~:text=Like%20most%20fruit%20plants%2C%20elderberries

Pennycross Resource Network. (2019). *Pennycress history.* Western Illinois University. https://www.wiu.edu/pennycress/history/index.php

Pesaturo, J. (2014, September 5). *Foraging aronia berries, wild super food.* Our One Acre Farm. https://ouroneacrefarm.com/2014/09/05/foraging-aronia-berries/

Petruzzelo, M. (n.d.). *Amaranth description, species, & nutrition.* Encyclopedia Britannica. https://www.britannica.com/plant/Amaranthus

Philadelphia Orchard Project. (2020, April 22). *Japanese knotweed: Edible, medicinal, invasive!* Philadelphia Orchard Project. https://www.phillyorchards.org/2020/04/22/japanese-knotweed-edible-medicinal-invasive/#:~:text=Mature%20shoots%20are%20much%20tougher

Philly Orchards. (2019, September 13). *Plant spotlight: Chokeberry (aronia).* Philadelphia Orchard Project. https://www.phillyorchards.org/2019/09/13/plant-spotlight-chokeberry-aronia/

Phlorum. (2021, February 20). *Plants that look like Japanese knotweed: Plants mistaken for knotweed.* Phlorum. https://www.phlorum.com/japanese-knotweed/plants-that-look-like-japanese-knotweed/

Plants For A Future. (n.d.-a). *Amphicarpaea bracteata Hog peanut, American hog peanut.* PFAF Plant Database. Retrieved July 14, 2022, from https://pfaf.org/user/plant.aspx?latinname=Amphicarpaea+bracteata

Plants For A Future. (n.d.-b). *Hemerocallis fulva common day lily, orange daylily, tawny daylily, double daylily.* PFAF Plant Database. Retrieved July 14, 2022, from https://pfaf.org/user/plant.aspx?LatinName=Hemerocallis+fulva

Poetry Foundation. (2020, March 5). *Preludes by T. S. Eliot.* Poetry Foundation. https://www.poetryfoundation.org/poems/44214/preludes-56d22338dc954

Putman, D. H., Oplinger, E. S., Doll, J. D., & Schulte, E. M. (2022, July 15). *Amaranth.* Perdue University. https://hort.purdue.edu/newcrop/afcm/amaranth.html

Raver, E. (2006, December 5). *Common plantain.* Bellarmine. https://www.bellarmine.edu/faculty/drobinson/CommonPlantain.asp

Ray-admin. (2022). *Sheeps sorrel, red sorrel, sourweed, field sorrel, Rumex acetosella.* Wild Food UK. https://www.wildfooduk.com/edible-wild-plants/sheeps-sorrel/

Rejba, A. (2020, May 14). *Off grid communities around the world—the complete guide.* The Smart Survivalist. https://www.thesmartsurvivalist.com/off-grid-communities-around-the-world-the-complete-guide/

Robbins, O. (2022, February 18). *What is amaranth? History, benefits, and uses.* Food Revolution Network. https://foodrevolution.org/blog/what-is-amaranth/

Roberts, M. (2012). *My 100 favorite herbs.* Struik Nature.

Roberts, M., & Roberts, S. (2015). *100 new herbs.* Struik Nature.

Rose, L. (2017, September 20). *How to forage for chicory this fall.* Growing up Herbal. https://growingupherbal.com/forage-for-chicory/

Sanders, A. (2013, August 19). *Lonicera sempervirens (trumpet honeysuckle): Go botany.* Native Plant Trust. https://gobotany.nativeplanttrust.org/species/lonicera/sempervirens/

Selinger, H. (2021, August 24). *5 wild grains you can cook with.* Modern Farmer. https://modernfarmer.com/2021/08/wild-grains-cooking/

Shmurak, S. (2020, March 12). *Elderberry identification and foraging tips.* HealthyGreenSavvy. https://www.healthygreensavvy.com/elderberry-identification/

Sinclair, K. (2019, August 7). *Five foraging facts with wild food stories.* Leanne Townsend Society. https://www.societyaberdeen.co.uk/food-drink/five-foraging-facts-with-wild-food-stories-leanne-townsend/

Smirch, J. (2021, March 31). *Marsh marigold, or perhaps not?.* Beyond Your Back Door. https://beyondyourbackdoor.net/2021/03/31/marsh-marigold-or-perhaps-not/#:~:text=Both%20Marsh%20Marigold%20and%20Lesser

Specialty Produce. (n.d.-a). *Field garlic.* Specialty Produce. Retrieved July 14, 2022, from https://specialtyproduce.com/produce/Field_Garlic_17295.php#:~:text=Description%2FTaste

Specialty Produce. (n.d.-b). *Sorghum bicolor.* Specialty Produce. Retrieved July 14, 2022, from https://specialtyproduce.com/produce/sorghum_bicolor_13168.php

Specialty Produce. (2022). *Japanese knotweed.* Specialty Produce. https://specialtyproduce.com/produce/Japanese_Knotweed_12189.php

Stephenson, K. (2021a). *Arrowhead: Pictures, flowers, leaves & identification Sagittaria latifolia.* Edible WIld Food. https://www.ediblewildfood.com/arrowhead.aspx

Stephenson, K. (2021b). *Common burdock, lesser burdock, Arctium minus, Arctium lappa.* Wild Food UK. https://www.wildfooduk.com/edible-wild-plants/burdock/

Stephenson, K. (2021c). *Field pennycress: Pictures, flowers, leaves & identification Thlaspi arvense.* Edible Wild Food. https://www.ediblewildfood.com/field-pennycress.aspx

Stephenson, K. (2021d). *Lamb's quarters: Pictures, flowers, leaves & identification Chenopodium album.* Edible Wild Food. https://www.ediblewildfood.com/lambs-quarters.aspx

Stephenson, K. (2021e). *Marsh marigold: Pictures, flowers, leaves & identification Caltha palustris.* Edible Wild Food. https://www.ediblewildfood.com/marsh-marigold.aspx

Stephenson, K. (2021f). *Nannyberry: Identification, leaves, bark & habitat Viburnum lentago.* Edible Wild Food. https://www.ediblewildfood.com/nannyberry.aspx#:~:text=in%20the%20autumn.-

Stephenson, K. (2021g). *Purslane: Pictures, flowers, leaves & identification Portulaca oleracea.* Edible Wild Food. https://www.ediblewildfood.com/purslane.aspx

Stephenson, K. (2021h). *Sheep sorrel: Pictures, flowers, leaves & identification Rumex acetosella.* Edible Wild Food. https://www.ediblewildfood.com/sheep-sorrel.aspx

Survival-manual.com. (n.d.). *Arrowhead wild edible plants for survival.* Survival-manual.-com. Retrieved July 14, 2022, from https://www.survival-manual.com/edible-plants/arrowhead.php

Swart, Z. (2022). Sheep's Sorrel. Mountain Herb Estate Nursery. https://herbgarden.-co.za/mountainherb/article.php?tag=SheepsSorrel

Sweet, H. (2020, May 19). *Evening primrose, a nutritious and medicinal garden favorite.* Eat the Planet. https://eattheplanet.org/evening-primrose-a-nutritious-and-medicinal-garden-favorite/#:~:text=You%20can%20eat%20the%20flowers

Sweetser, R. (2022, February 28). *Shamrocks and four-leaf clovers: What's the difference?* Almanac. https://www.almanac.com/clover-shamrocks-and-oxalis-whats-differ ence#:https://www.almanac.com/clover-shamrocks-and-oxalis-whats-difference

Sycamore, S. (2018, May 9). *How to identify lambsquarters—foraging for edible wild spinach.* Good Life Revival. https://thegoodliferevival.com/blog/lambsquarters-wild-spinach

Tentree.com. (2017, October 22). *6 off-grid, sustainable communities that live harmoniously with the environment.* The Environmentor. https://blog.tentree.com/6-off-grid-sustainable-communities-that-live-harmoniously-with-the-environment/

Tesolin, I. (2020, March 16). *Lambsquarters identification: How to forage this edible wild plant.* RusticWise. https://rusticwise.com/lambsquarters-identification/

Tesolin, J. (2020, September 24). *Foraging: How to eat the cattail plant + 5 tasty cattail recipes.* RusticWise. https://rusticwise.com/how-to-eat-the-cattail-plant/

Texas Wildflower Center. (n.d.). *Tillia Americana.* Lady Bird Johnson Wildflower Center —The University of Texas at Austin. https://www.wildflower.org/plants/result.php? id_plant=TIAM

Thayer, S. (2006). *The forager's harvest (2nd ed.).* Forager's harvest. https://www.pdf-drive.com/the-foragers-harvest-a-guide-to-identifying-harvesting-and-preparing-edible-wild-plants-c163383641.html

Thayer, S. (2022, April 1). *Wild parsnip: Harvesting, cooking, and safety.* Forager Chef. https://foragerchef.com/wild-parsnip-harvesting-cooking-and-safety/#:~:text=Just%20like%20garden%20parsnip%2C%20there

The Joy Of Plants. (n.d.). *Honeysuckle.* The Joy of Plants. Retrieved July 14, 2022, from https://www.thejoyofplants.co.uk/honeysuckle#:~:text=The%20-name%20%27honeysuckle%27%20is%20derived

The Scotts Company. (1995). *Scotts guide to the identification of grasses.* The Scotts Company.

360 Farms. (2022). *Elderberry history and research.* 360 Farms. https://www.360okfarms.com/portfolio/elderberry-history-and-research/#:~:text=Elderber-ry%20has%20a%20well%20documented

Trimboli, S. (2019, May 21). *Common evening primrose (Oenothera biennis).* Backyard Ecol-ogy. https://www.backyardecology.net/common-evening-primrose/

Trull, S. (n.d.). *Yellow marsh marigold.* US Forest Service. Retrieved July 14, 2022, from https://www.fs.fed.us/wildflowers/plant-of-the-week/caltha_palustris.shtml#:~:text=Marsh%20marigold%20has%20glossy%20green

TWC Staff. (2013). *Typha latifolia.* Lady Bird Johnson Wildflower Center—The Univer-sity of Texas at Austin. https://www.wildflower.org/plants/result.php?id_plant=tyla

TWC Staff. (2019, January 24). *Lonicera sempervirens.* Lady Bird Johnson Wildflower Center—The University of Texas at Austin. https://www.wildflower.org/plants/result.php?id_plant=lose

United Nations. (2021). *68% of the world population projected to live in urban areas by 2050, says UN.* United Nations Department of Economic and Social Development. https://www.un.org/sw/desa/68-world-population-projected-live-urban-areas-2050-says-un

University of Maine. (n.d.). *Plant description and habitat of aronia (black chokeberry).* University of Maine Cooperative Extension: Agriculture. https://extension.umaine.edu/agriculture/aronia/plant-description-and-habitat/

University of Wyoming. (n.d.). *Forage identification—Glossary.* University of Wyoming. Retrieved July 14, 2022, from https://www.uwyo.edu/plantsciences/uwplant/forages/glossary.html

UPMC. (2020, February 19). *What are the benefits of elderberry?* UPMC HealthBeat. https://share.upmc.com/2020/02/benefits-of-elderberry/#:~:text=One%20cup%20of%20elderberries%20contains

Utah State University. (n.d.). *Broadleaf cattail.* Utah State Extension. Retrieved July 14, 2022, from https://extension.usu.edu/rangeplants/grasses-and-grasslikes/broadleaf-cattail#:~:text=Growth%20Characteristics%3A%20Broadleaf%20cattail%20is

Vorderbruggen, M. (n.d.-a). *Common evening primrose.* Foraging Texas. Retrieved July 14, 2022, from https://www.foragingtexas.com/2011/12/common-evening-primrose.html

Vorderbruggen, M. (n.d.-b). *Curled dock, yellow dock.* Foraging Texas. Retrieved July 14, 2022, from https://www.foragingtexas.com/2008/08/dock.html

Vorderbruggen, M. (2017). *Basswood/linden.* Foraging Texas.https://www.foragingtexas.com/2008/08/basswoodlinden_20.html

Vorderbruggen, M. (2022). *Chicory.* Foraging Texas. https://www.foragingtexas.com/2008/08/chicory.html

Walker, C. (2020, May 27). *Edible roots, stems, and bulbs.* Penn State Extension. https://extension.psu.edu/edible-roots-stems-and-bulbs

Walliser, J. (2016, June 21). *Grow fiddlehead ferns for market.* Hobby Farms. https://www.hobbyfarms.com/grow-fiddlehead-ferns-for-market/#:~:text=Growing%20Fiddleheads

Washington Post Lifestyle. (2002, June 19). *How to pick and prepare purslane.* Washington Post. https://www.washingtonpost.com/archive/lifestyle/food/2002/06/19/how-to-pick-and-prepare-purslane/5109fc88-1282-4072-8539-a2321798ac2b/

Watson, S. (2022). *Bartenders' guide to foraging: Honeysuckle.* Difford's Guide. https://www.diffordsguide.com/encyclopedia/1695/bws/bartenders-guide-to-foraging-honeysuckle

Web MD. (n.d.). *Ostrich Fern: Overview, uses, side effects, precautions, interactions, dosing and reviews.* WebMD. https://www.webmd.com/vitamins/ai/ingredientmono-492/ostrich-fern

Weed Science Society of America. (2022a). *Common dandelion—the lion's tooth.* WSSA. https://wssa.net/wp-content/themes/WSSA/WorldOfWeeds/dandelion.html

Weed Science Society of America. (2022b). *Common lambsquarters.* WSSA. https://wssa.net/wp-content/themes/WSSA/WorldOfWeeds/lambsquarters.html#:~:text=Common%20lambsquarters%20grew%20in%20Britain

Weed Science Society of America. (2022c). *Common purslane.* WSSA. https://wssa.net/wp-content/themes/WSSA/WorldOfWeeds/purslane.html

Weed Science Society of America. (2022d). *Field pennycross—the stinkweed.* WSSA. https://wssa.net/wp-content/themes/WSSA/WorldOfWeeds/pennycress.html#:~:text=ETYMOLOGY%20AND%20HISTORY&text=Field%20pennycress%20was%20collected%20at

Weed Science Society of America. (2022e). *White man's foot—broadleaf plantain.* WSSA. https://wssa.net/wp-content/themes/WSSA/WorldOfWeeds/whitemansfoot.html

Wentworth, J. (2013, March 20). *Gardening with edible and useful native shrubs.* WNPS. https://www.wnps.org/blog/gardening-with-edible-and-useful-native-shrubs

West Virginia University. (n.d.). *Common chickweed.* West Virginia Extension. Retrieved July 14, 2022, from https://extension.wvu.edu/lawn-gardening-pests/weeds/common-chickweed#:~:text=Chickweed%20likely%20got%20its%20name

White, D. A. (2022, March 8). Parsnip nutrition facts and health benefits. Verywell Fit. https://www.verywellfit.com/parsnips-nutrition-facts-4177762

Wikipedia. (2020a, May 14). *Typha.* Wikipedia. https://en.wikipedia.org/wiki/Typha

Wikipedia. (2020b, June 9). *Tilia americana.* Wikipedia. https://en.wikipedia.org/wiki/Tilia_americana

Wikipedia. (2021a, March 24). *Locust tree.* Wikipedia. https://en.m.wikipedia.org/wiki/Locust_tree#:~:text=%22Locust%22%20comes%20from%20the%20Latin

Wikipedia. (2021b, December 14). *Lonicera sempervirens.* Wikipedia. https://en.wikipedia.org/wiki/Lonicera_sempervirens

Wikipedia. (2022a, April 16). *Matteuccia.* Wikipedia. https://en.wikipedia.org/wiki/Matteuccia

Wikipedia. (2022b, April 17). *Fragaria virginiana.* Wikipedia. https://en.wikipedia.org/wiki/Fragaria_virginiana

Wikipedia. (2022c, May 5). *Oenothera biennis.* Wikipedia. https://en.wikipedia.org/wiki/Oenothera_biennis

Wikipedia Contributors. (2019, November 21). *Prunus virginiana.* Wikipedia; Wikimedia Foundation. https://en.wikipedia.org/wiki/Prunus_virginiana

Wild Food UK. (n.d.). *Common burdock, lesser burdock, Arctium minus, Arctium lappa.* Wild Food UK. https://www.wildfooduk.com/edible-wild-plants/burdock/

Wild Plant Guides. (n.d.). *A-Z Foraging Glossary. The language of plants.* Wild Plant Guides. Retrieved July 14, 2022, from https://wildplantguides.com/foraging-glossary/

Wild Plants Guide. (2021, May 3). *How to identify marsh marigold (Caltha palustris) Ranunculaceae family.* Wild Plant Guides. https://wildplantguides.com/2021/05/03/how-to-identify-marsh-marigold/#:https://wildplantguides.com/2021/05/03/how-

REFERENCES

to-identify-marsh-marigold/#:~:text=You%20can%20identify%20marsh%20marigold

Williams, M. (2929, April 2). *Flowering currant—identification, distribution, edibility, recipes*. Galloway Wild Foods. https://gallowaywildfoods.com/flowering-currant-identification-distribution-edibility-recipes/

Wisconsin Food Forest. (2022, March 28). *Nannyberry (Viburnum lentago)*. Wisconsin Food Forest. https://www.wisconsinfoodforests.com/nannyberry-viburnum-lentago/

Wisconsin Horticulture. (n.d.). *Dandelion, Taraxacum officinale*. Wisconsin Horticulture. https://hort.extension.wisc.edu/articles/dandelion-taraxacum-officinale/

Woodland Trust. (n.d.). *Honeysuckle (Lonicera periclymenum)*. Woodland Trust. https://www.woodlandtrust.org.uk/trees-woods-and-wildlife/plants/wild-flowers/honeysuckle/

Yee, V., & Goodman, P. S. (2021, March 24). *Suez Canal blocked after giant container ship gets stuck*. The New York Times. https://www.nytimes.com/2021/03/24/world/middleeast/suez-canal-blocked-ship.html#:~:text=The%20ship%2C%20stretching%20more%20than

IMAGE CREDITS

Atik Sugiwara, botanical sketches of aronia berry, black locust, black-berries, chickweed, curly dock, hog peanut, Japanese knotweed, nannyberry, parsnip, purslane, Siberian elm, wild garlic.

Artist contact information:
https://www.instagram.com/atik.sugiwara/
https://www.fiverr.com/atiksugiwara

Andyballard. (n.d.). *Elderflower basket* [Image]. Pixabay. Retrieved October 27, 2022, from https://pixabay.com/photos/elderflowers-english-countryside-1164950/

Chikilino. (n.d.). *Sunset trees* [Image]. Pixabay. Retrieved October 27, 2022, from https://pixabay.com/photos/field-trees-nature-sunset-4452538/

Cocoparisienne. (n.d.). *Wild mushroom basket* [Image]. Pixabay. Retrieved October 27, 2022, from https://pixabay.com/photos/mushrooms-edible-mushrooms-2678385/

Coleur. (n.d.). *Red clover* [Image]. Pixabay. Retrieved October 27, 2022, from https://pixabay.com/photos/clover-blossom-bloom-purple-3430247/

Falkenpost. (n.d.). *Grass prairie* [Image]. Pixabay. Retrieved October 27, 2022, from https://pixabay.com/photos/wyoming-prairie-hulett-usa-america-1633631/

GPoulsen. (n.d.). *Mountain elk* [Image]. Pixabay. Retrieved October 27, 2022, from https://pixabay.com/photos/elk-wildlife-nature-outdoors-banff-7068143/

Jonathansautter. (n.d.). *Wildflowers at sunset* [Image]. Pixabay. Retrieved October 27,

2022, from https://pixabay.com/photos/meadow-sunset-nature-blade-of-grass-811339/

Kapa65. (n.d.). *Forest path* [Image]. Pixabay. Retrieved October 27, 2022, from https://pixabay.com/photos/forest-trees-forest-path-2735623/

KristineLejniece. (n.d.). *Picnic flower book* [Image]. Pixabay. Retrieved October 27, 2022, from https://pixabay.com/photos/book-flowers-forest-bouquet-garden-2550168/

Lake canoe. (n.d.). [Image]. Pixabay. Retrieved October 27, 2022, from https://pixabay.com/photos/guyana-sky-clouds-lake-stream-80836/

Maxmann. (n.d.). *Linden tree seeds* [Image]. Pixabay. Retrieved October 27, 2022, from https://pixabay.com/photos/linden-tree-tree-linden-seeds-fall-1719450/

Mozlase. (n.d.). *Red currant cup* [Image]. Pixabay. Retrieved October 27, 2022, from https://pixabay.com/photos/berries-currant-red-3837889/

Ulieo. (n.d.). *Parsnip basket* [Image]. Pixabay. Retrieved October 27, 2022, from https://pixabay.com/photos/parsnips-root-vegetable-parsley-root-3860993/

Vladvictoria. (n.d.). *Child with basket* [Image]. Pixabay. Retrieved October 27, 2022, from https://pixabay.com/photos/easter-egg-hunt-child-spring-4143537/

All other images used under license from shutterstock.com